TRICIA KI...

MAKING IT

HOW TO HANDLE LOVE

PAN

This book is dedicated to all the young people, particularly *MIZZ* readers, who have entrusted me with their problems. I hope it goes some way towards answering their many questions.

First published 1989 by Macdonald & Company (Publishers) Limited

This Pan edition published 1993 by Pan Macmillan Children's Books
a division of Pan Macmillan Publishers Limited
Cavaye Place London SW10 9PG
and Basingstoke

Associated companies throughout the world

ISBN 0 330 32863 8

Copyright © Tricia Kreitman 1989, 1993

The right of Tricia Kreitman to be identified as
author of this work has been asserted by her in accordance
with the Copyright, Designs and Patents Act 1988.

Illustrations by Jane Eccles

All rights reserved. No reproduction, copy or transmission
of this publication may be made without written permission.
No paragraph of this publication may be reproduced, copied or
transmitted save with written permission or in accordance with
the provisions of the Copyright Act 1956 (as amended). Any
person who does any unauthorised act in relation to
this publication may be liable to criminal prosecution
and civil claims for damages.

1 3 5 7 9 8 6 4 2

A CIP catalogue record for this book is available from
the British Library

Phototypeset by Intype, London
Printed by Cox & Wyman Ltd, Reading

This book is sold subject to the condition that it shall not,
by way of trade or otherwise, be lent, re-sold, hired out,
or otherwise circulated without the publisher's prior consent
in any form of binding or cover other than that in which
it is published and without a similar condition including this
condition being imposed on the subsequent purchaser.

CONTENTS

Introduction — vii

Chapter One: What is love? — 1
Addicted to love – What the experts say

Chapter Two: Unlucky in love — 7
Not finding a partner – Where to go for help

Chapter Three: Sniggers and giggles — 15
What is homosexuality – Love and sex – Coming out

Chapter Four: A first date — 25
Asking someone out – What makes you decide – Nerves

Chapter Five: Breaking up — 32
How to cope – Ending a relationship – Becoming friends

Chapter Six: Staying together — 38
Parental approval – Jealousy and rows – Responsibilities

Chapter Seven: Approaching sex — 46
The ultimate cocktail – Coping with sex – Sex and the law

Chapter Eight: Sex – the mechanics and the fun — 54
Foreplay – Orgasms – The first time – Saying no

Chapter Nine: Contraception – the facts — 68
Where to get it – Types of contraception – Myths

Chapter Ten: Being pregnant — 80
Pregnancy tests – Telling people – Having the baby

Chapter Eleven: Sexual health — 93
Hygiene – Infections and cures – Getting help

CONTENTS

Chapter Twelve: HIV and AIDS — 101
What is it? – How do you get it? – Protection – Getting help

Chapter Thirteen: Sexual problems — 108
Sexual arousal – Getting help

Contacts — 126

Emergencies — 136

INTRODUCTION

If you ever find yourself lying awake at night worrying about love, wondering who on earth you can ask for help, then this book is for you.

Possibly the only positive aspect of AIDS becoming a fact of life is that these days we can all talk a bit more freely about sex. But a lot of that talk still stays very theoretical; when it comes to discussing our own emotions and sexuality, things get very difficult. Parents are confused and nervous about telling their kids 'the facts of life' and many opt out, hoping the school will take care of it for them. Some schools cope admirably but others, under severe financial and timetable pressure, and understandably worried about offending parents and governors, stick to the biology of rabbits and a few words about 'being careful'.

The old wives' tales that were there in my mother's time and in mine are still doing the rounds of teenagers today. Feelings of inadequacy and plain ignorance are still causing as many problems now as they did 40 years ago. But somehow we are supposed to know all about love and making love. The plain fact is that we don't.

It is very easy (and a real cop out) for adults to say 'plenty of time for worrying about that when you're older' or 'don't know what you're getting so worked up about, it's only puppy love'. They forget just how much it can hurt to be young and how desolate you can feel when love doesn't go the way you want it to.

As an Agony Aunt I receive about 500 letters a week ranging from the humorous to the tragic. Each person who writes considers their problem to be insurmountable and they write to me because they don't know who else to turn to. One letter I had recently seems to sum it all up.

INTRODUCTION

Dear Tricia,

Please can you help me because I feel that everyone knows things that I don't. I'm too embarrassed to talk to my parents or ask my teachers so can you tell me all about love, sex and all that stuff?

Love, sex and all that stuff is exactly what I'd like to get clear in this book.

My aim is to tell young people facts as well as explaining the implications and responsibilities of love and sexuality. Sex under the age of consent is illegal. I also happen to believe that it's wrong because of the physical and emotional dangers associated with it. But telling 14- and 15-year-olds (or even younger) that it's wrong won't stop them doing it. Neither will withdrawing contraceptive and advice services. It's been tried and it hasn't worked.

An understanding of the responsibilities and the dangers in a sexual relationship just might have some effect. And an awareness of their capacity for sexual arousal might help teenagers appreciate that intercourse isn't just the next step on from kissing and hugging and that loving can have many different ways of expression other than the 'bonking' that appears in the headlines.

Tricia Kreitman

CHAPTER ONE

What is love?

What is this thing called love?

Maybe I should be honest and admit straight away that I don't think I'm altogether sure what love is. I know there are people that I love and have loved but the experience of loving seems to have been a bit different every time. I loved my first boyfriend when I was 15 and I love the man I live with now. It's easy to say that I only thought I was in love all those years ago. But it seemed real enough at the time. And it certainly hurt enough when we split up.

So what is love? Does anyone know for sure? I listened to teenagers talking about their feelings on love and then had a look at what the 'experts' had to say about it.

Young people talking about love

'Love is feeling different. It's when you can't wait to see them or when you know that you're going to see them and you get a lovely warm feeling inside.'

'It's when you want to see someone every minute of every day and all the time there's this great warm feeling inside you, a kind of secret, and you only have to touch it with your mind, and think of the two of you together, for you to feel amazing.'

'You know you're in love when you can go and watch a sad film or telly programme and cry without feeling stupid. Sometimes he cries too or he just puts his arms round me and holds me. That's love.'

Talking to them, I got the strong impression that though boys and girls agreed on the basic symptoms of love – the all enveloping feeling of tenderness for someone – the boys saw it as something that would happen to them one day in the future. It was for 'settling down with' when they were 'grown up'. But the girls wanted it now. They were actively looking for love and expecting to be in love.

The girls were putting tremendous energy into yearning and longing. And seemed to have been doing so for quite a long time. When we talked about the early feelings of love, sometimes called crushes, many of them remembered those kind of feelings starting as early as 8 or 10. All the girls went on to say 'of course, it wasn't real love. I know that now.' But at the time they experienced it as love and I think it served as an important practice for a later, more mature, kind of loving.

Addicted to love

Not surprisingly, everyone who admitted to having been in love said they had enjoyed it. However it had ended, they still felt that the buzz and the high while they were in love had made it all worthwhile. (In a minute I'll tell you what the experts have to say about that.) Because it felt so good, many of them seemed to get addicted to being in love. One girl was very frank about this.

'I know that I like being in love and I'm aware that sometimes I talk myself into it. I meet someone at a party or club and arrange to see him again. In the days before that happens I think about him a lot, try and remember his face, build up all sorts of fantasies about him. By the time I see him I'm already in love with him and there's probably not much that he could do to change my views on that. I suppose, in reality, I'm in love with my image of someone, not the real boy. But I never seem to realise that at the time. It's only later, looking back, that I see this guy and think "But that isn't who I was going out with, is it?"'

The whole world wants you to fall in love

If you look around at the world it seems that everybody and everything is conspiring to push you into someone's arms. There's all this pressure on you to become part of a couple and show off your love to the world.

Look at television ads, read teenage or women's magazines and watch any soap. The boy who drinks the 'in' lager gets the girl. The girl who wears the 'right' body spray gets the boy. A story has a 'happy' ending if the couple finish up in love. A sad ending is when someone is left on their own.

The moral of all this comes through loud and clear. If you're worth anything, they seem to be saying, if you're successful, you have someone who loves you. So to show the world that you're not a failure you've got to find that girl or that boy, and you've got to hang on to them.

'I did all the chatting, the phoning, the suggesting that we went out to a party or a film and he just went along with it. Oh, he said he loved me sometimes, when I asked him, and he always got very amorous (you know, all over me) when it was time to say good night but he never did anything or even said anything remotely interesting. Never really said very much at all, I suppose! By the time I'd realised the relationship was all one-sided, my side, it was too late. I'd been telling everyone what a wonderful guy he was, how lucky I was, trying to make all my friends jealous. I could hardly turn round and admit the truth, could I? So we just went on like that. It was easier than being on my own. We'd probably still be like that today if he hadn't gone and fallen in love with someone. Funny thing is, I really miss him.'

Sometimes the pressure to pair up comes from much closer to home.

'My parents, they're always asking, "Have you got a girlfriend? When are you going to bring her home? Did you meet anyone at the disco?" Then when I do go out with someone the next thing they're asking me is "Are you in love with her?" As though I'd say yes, even if I was!'

And there is also the unseen but relentless pressure from our friends. 'Who are you going out with? Who is she seeing?' It's the biggest topic of conversation; especially on Monday mornings. If all you did was sit at home and watch telly or a video you can't help but feel a failure but 'keeping up with the crowd' still isn't a good enough reason for going out with someone you don't care for or have no interest in.

Even if all your friends spend the entire English lesson writing their boyfriends' names all over the desks, you shouldn't feel there is anything wrong with you for not having someone you feel that way about. Different people's lives go at different paces and it could be that you aren't ready yet for that sort of relationship. (There is more about this in the next chapter 'Unlucky in love'.)

Sometimes, maybe often, all this pressure's too much and people do fall in love for the wrong reasons. After all, if everyone and everything you read is saying that love's such a great thing, and then someone comes along, someone quite nice that is, who really appears to like you, you'd have to be terribly sure of yourself to be able to say, 'No, this isn't what I want, this isn't right for me.'

WHAT IS LOVE?

The right stuff

Not everyone, thankfully, has bad experiences of love. Some people seem to have really good relationships going. Some of them had been through a very intense phase of falling in love and now saw something calmer and more stable growing out of it. Others found themselves falling in love almost unexpectedly with someone who'd just been a good friend.

'I've known him for ages, we all went round in a crowd together but I'd never fancied him. Then one day he asked me out. At first I thought "you've got to be kidding" that wasn't what I wanted. But then I thought I'd give it a go. I wasn't seeing anyone else and there wasn't any harm in it. And I really enjoyed myself. We just had a great laugh and when he did kiss me it seemed natural. We've been together ever since and I know that the love we feel for each other is really good because underneath we're friends too.'

'I fancied her friend really, she was the blonde one, the one everyone wanted to get off with. Liz was much quieter, so quiet you didn't really notice her in a crowd. Anyway me and my mate managed to get together with the two of them and of course he got off with the friend. So I was left with Liz. I decided to make the best out of a bad job and then I found that when she was on her own she could talk. And she was funny. What's more, when she wasn't standing beside her friend I could see she was really quite pretty. It's gone on from there. I don't know now what I'd do without her.'

So what do the experts say?

One of the most interesting things I discovered is that there's a sound physical reason for us to feel the way we do when we're in love. You know the high, buzzy feeling you get when you don't want to sleep or eat and you feel as if the whole world is lit up? Well, when you fall in love the body produces a very special chemical called phenylethylamine which in turn has the effect of producing adrenaline. This rushes around in the blood stream stimulating you and particularly your brain. It's as though all your reflexes go into hyper-drive and you get the tight, tense feeling that something very exciting is going to happen, even something scary, but whatever it is you're strung up and breathless and ready for it.

People often say they can tell when someone's in love and they could be right. It gives a sudden boost to your self-confidence but all the extra energy also makes your skin glow and you move and even talk in a slightly different way.

That's the physical side of falling in love but there are also many psychological theories of what it does to you and how it affects your life.

Adolescence is a time of exploration and development of self-identity. When you bury yourself totally in a relationship with some bloke or girl that your parents and family can't stand, you're also saying 'But look, I'm a separate person to you, I'm able to do this and I have a right to do it if I choose.' You're exploring and pushing back boundaries and preparing the path for breaking away from the family and becoming an adult in your own right.

So the next time someone complains that you're 'mooning about in love' tell them to stop interfering and leave you alone with your struggle for self-identity!

CHAPTER TWO

Unlucky in love

I have never met anyone who didn't at some time feel that they were desperately unlucky in love. The whole business of dating and romancing is full of ups and downs and there are bound to be bad times when you feel that fate is against you and you're never going to find that one special person.

There are two main categories of people who think they qualify for the title of 'Unlucky in love'. The first are the ones who've never had a boy or girlfriend and feel that they never will. The second are those who do have relationships but each of them ends badly, often with a kind of destructive pattern repeating itself over and over again. So let's look at the different types of problem that we have here.

'I've never had a boy/girlfriend. All my friends have got someone special so what's wrong with me?'

There probably isn't anything wrong with you at all. It may just be that you aren't ready yet to have a relationship. Different people seem to start dating at different times and what's right for one 14- or 15-year-old can be too early and just plain wrong for another. Of course it's hard when all your friends are going out with someone and you're fed up with sitting at home alone or being the gooseberry on the end of the row, but try to hold on to the idea that it won't last for ever.

It's hard to ignore the pressure to conform but the fact that all your friends are doing something doesn't mean that you're a freak for not joining in. Different people have different reasons for being late starters.

For example:

The late developer

The big landmark between childhood and the beginning of adulthood is when a girl starts to menstruate (have periods) and when a boy starts to ejaculate, i.e. produce sperm from his penis. This shouldn't be mistaken as an order from on high to go out and have sex. Nor should sexual attraction be mistaken for Love with a capital L (in other words the REAL THING). It's similar, but real love involves a growing and strengthening relationship. And that needs more than the odd spot of maturity as well as the ability to communicate with someone else.

Some people feel the attraction of the opposite sex at 12 or 13 and others don't get the slightest twinge until many years later. They feel they ought to be out there fancying people like mad but it just doesn't seem to happen.

When all's said and done, the hormones that cause you to feel physically attracted to someone are just plain chemicals. Some people's bodies develop those chemicals quicker than others. Give your body time and it will get there in the end.

The loner

The loner doesn't have a boy or girlfriend but he (or she) doesn't have any other close friends either. He doesn't necessarily feel that

UNLUCKY IN LOVE

he's missing out in this and he probably keeps himself quite busy in fairly solitary activities. He might be a bit of a swot or he might be intensely involved with some kind of hobby. Or perhaps he's just a dreamer. But somehow he never seems to make the right sort of close contact necessary for a friendship to grow. One way out is to find himself a group of people with the same kind of interests and gradually develop his social skills.

Some loners take several weeks to learn how to say 'hello'. They're not naturally rude, it just doesn't occur to them to talk to other people. But once they get the hang of it they discover that having friends is quite nice after all and the next thing they know they find they're talking to girls as though they were actually human beings. And once you can talk to a girl comfortably as a friend it doesn't take too much to pluck up the courage to ask her out.

The coward

The coward's problem is that he can't bring himself to ask someone out. Or if she's a girl, she isn't able to say 'yes' when someone asks her out. The coward can imagine just how bad rejection would feel and every time he looks at someone he fancies he sees a sort of video pre-play of how it would be if she said 'no'.

The girl coward is scared of what would happen. So, even if someone asks her and she really likes the look of them, she won't be able to say 'yes' because she's sure (in her own mind) that they can't be serious or they'd change their minds once they got to know her.

The coward's life is usually made even more of a misery by his or her friends. They're always there, egging them on to *do* something. 'Go on, ask her. Why don't you say yes?' Luckily, in most cases, the situation resolves itself when they meet someone who's so special that they forget all about their nervousness.

The hunchback

The hunchback blames the sorry state of their social lives on one particular thing. It isn't usually a real hunchback. Sometimes it's a nose that's too big or the wrong shape. Sometimes it's sticking-out ears. Sometimes they're too fat or too thin or one breast is larger than the other or they've got bad breath or they don't know how to kiss. The hunchback is so obsessed with this defect in him/herself that they can't possibly believe that other people aren't aware of it.

The best advice I can give to the hunchbacks is for them to look at themselves very carefully in a full-length mirror. What can be changed and what can't? If it's a question of hair or skin or body shape then an improved diet, more exercise, fresh air and a trip to the hairdresser or to the doctor for help with acne will start to make them feel better. It won't make the problem go away overnight but the fact that they're doing something positive to tackle it should improve their self-confidence and morale.

But if the problem is one breast being larger than the other or a bulbous nose or being too tall or too short they have to face up to the fact that that's how they are. But a crooked nose is only on the outside and it will only affect their personality (i.e. what's on the inside) if they let it. Learning to like themselves can be difficult but if they can't do it, no one else will.

The perfectionist

The perfectionist would certainly love to have a boy or girlfriend. They dream about it endlessly but somehow no one who's quite right ever drifts into their range of vision. Even if they look okay at first sight, there's always something a little bit wrong on closer inspection. The trouble with the perfectionist is that they're mixing up real life with their fantasy world.

If you think there's a chance that you might be setting your sights too high, try to forget about love and romance for a while. Look at the people around you and set yourself the project of getting to know them a bit better. Okay, so the guy you see on the bus every day (you know, the one who always smiles at you) isn't your ideal man but he still might be a nice guy. Try talking to him. Find out more about him and I think you'll be surprised at how interesting an 'ordinary' person can be. Don't lead him on. You're not playing any flirting games here. You're just learning to make friends.

Practise this for a few weeks and you might find that your vision of 'what's right for you' has changed.

'That's all very well but it's not that I have trouble meeting someone, it's just that every relationship ends the same way – badly'

Psychologists have a theory that everyone lives their lives according to a sort of pre-set script. These scripts are a result of early childhood, family problems and attitudes and self-image. The script influences the way you feel about yourself and how you act and behave. This in turn has an effect on other people who are close to you and they tend to respond to you in a particular way as well. The majority of people get by in an okay sort of way but some people develop a very destructive script and they get stuck in a series of relationships where they're used or even abused. They see no end to it as each new relationship confirms for them the feeling that somehow they 'deserve' what's happening.

Agony Aunts get a lot of letters from people with this problem.

'Everytime I start to go out with a girl I think they're great. The more I get to know them the better I like them. And they like me. Everything's all right until I've told them I love them and then they seem to run a mile. How come those three little words make such a difference?'

'I went out with my last boyfriend for years. He was on drugs and always in and out of trouble but he tried to give them up and I felt I was really helping him towards this. He knew how much it upset me and he did try for my sake. But he didn't make it and eventually he drifted away. My parents don't like my new boyfriend any more than they did the last. He's been in prison though he's going straight now. Everyone's biased against him but I know that my love is going to help him win through.'

'I don't think I'm ever going to find anyone normal. I've had three boyfriends and in the end they've always become violent. I know they love me, they say it and I can feel it, but somehow I always seem to do something wrong and it ends up with them shouting at me and hitting me. I try to be very careful because I don't want to upset them and I know it's always my fault but I always end up making a mistake. If only I could work out what it is and how to keep them happy, everything would be okay.'

These are all extreme examples but they aren't, by any means, uncommon. The first person wondered why telling his girlfriends that he loved them made them run away. It probably wasn't just the three little words, it was more likely what went with them. I suspect that he tried to smother them with his love and also demanded too much love back in return. The girls just weren't able to cope with it or to deliver what was expected.

The second person was obviously attracted to lame dogs. She wanted someone she could rescue and she enjoyed the feeling of being able (or at least trying) to influence someone's life.

In a way, she was trying to mother them. It may be that this pattern of loving domination and 'saving them from themselves' is the only type of loving she's ever seen. In that case, it's no wonder that she deliberately seeks out men who fulfil the poor little victim role so that she can rescue them. The fact that she never does seem to rescue them and ends up alone and hurt doesn't ever really filter into her consciousness.

The other girl was in a very dangerous situation. She wasn't surprised when men were violent towards her. She even felt that she deserved it. Possibly she had been a scapegoat in her family at home. Her parents may not have hit her, but they may have made her feel that she was always the one in the wrong. Again, that's an experience of family life and loving, so she translates that into her relationship to mean that if someone hits her they also love her. This girl is in danger and if she doesn't break out of her script she could end up badly hurt.

Ask yourself if there is some way you can change your script. What are the factors that make each relationship go wrong? Is it the partners you choose? Is it how you feel about yourself and what you deserve from life? Or is it the way you think that relationships ought to go?

Sometimes, talking this through with a sympathetic friend can help you sort things out. But often that isn't enough and then you may need professional counselling in order to move on in your life and have a chance of creating a successful relationship.

Where to go for help

NB. All addresses and phone numbers can be found in the 'Contacts' section at the end of the book.

If you feel unhappy about your ability to form a relationship or are worried about the way that a particular relationship or relationships in general seem to go for you then it's always a good idea to talk to a professional counsellor.

Look in the front of your phone book or *Thomson Directory* under 'counselling' for details of local young people's counselling services. Most of them are free and many of them don't require you to make an appointment. Some also offer telephone helplines. Help is also available either through **Brook Advisory Centres** or by contacting **Youth Access**. Brook has several branches in London and other cities and Youth Access acts as a referral system so that you write to them with an s.a.e. and they let you know where your nearest counselling service is. Most of these organisations offer free counselling if you are under 25.

You can also get very good help from **RELATE**, which used to be called the National Marriage Guidance Council. They don't insist on seeing couples and they don't mind whether you're married or not. If you've got a relationship problem and you can't find a specific Youth Counsellor then you can find the address of your nearest RELATE office by looking under Marriage Guidance in the phone directory or by asking at your local library.

If the problem is more one of making friends and just getting out and meeting people it's worth considering dating agencies and clubs. Most of these have a minimum age limit and it may be that you have to wait until you're 18 before joining (by which time, of course, the problem will have probably disappeared) but there's nothing to be ashamed of in using their facilities. People poke a lot of fun at marriage bureaux and dating agencies but I suspect that many more couples came together because of them than we will ever know.

But remember, always take the basic safety precautions of never meeting someone in an isolated place and making sure that you can always walk out and get home on your own if you don't like the look of them.

Some people, either from being at a single sex school or in a job with few other young people, find it very difficult to meet anyone at all. That's where clubs and groups come in. I know it's corny old Agony Aunts' advice suggesting that you should go and join a local evening class, but it does work. Obviously a girl's got more chance of meeting men if she joins Car Maintenance and vice versa if a boy joins Cookery but even if you don't meet the love of your dreams you're likely to make some good friends of all different ages.

Your local library is the best place to find out about these classes and they should also keep a list of local clubs and associations.

CHAPTER THREE

Sniggers and giggles

When I was writing this book I interviewed a lot of young people, of both sexes, from the ages of 14 to 22. In my introduction to each group I went over what I hoped to cover in my book. As soon as I mentioned homosexuality there would be a ripple of embarrassed laughter. When this had happened to me a few times I started asking the groups why they were laughing. I didn't get much reply, though one or two braver individuals said surely I wasn't serious including gays and lesbians in the book and if so, what did it have to do with them anyway?

I was very surprised by all this. It may have been naive of me but I assumed that young people today had a more enlightened view of homosexuality than the older generation. What surprised me most of all was that these people weren't reacting against fear of AIDS (for more about this see the chapter on HIV and AIDS) or as a result of the modern media-encouraged phobia of homosexuality. They simply seemed to see the subject as a kind of smutty joke. All of them saw homosexuals as a race apart; something so strange and possibly frightening that they had never even tried to understand it.

So what is all this homo/hetero stuff?

A homosexual is a man or a woman who is attracted exclusively to his or her own sex. Male homosexuals are known as gays, although people who are scared or threatened by the idea of homosexuality often call them names such as queers, poofs, woofters, etc. Female homosexuals are often called lesbians, gays and dikes.

The 'normal' pattern of life is that males and females have sex, reproduce and continue the species. This 'straight' sex is called heterosexuality. In other words a heterosexual is someone who is attracted to the opposite sex.

Just to make things even more complicated, there's the third category of bisexuality. This refers to people who are attracted to both sexes!

What causes it?

There are many different theories but no one is 100 per cent sure. Some researchers are working on the idea that it may have a physical or genetic cause. This is obviously controversial.

Can it be cured?

Again, lots of therapists have had a go at curing homosexuals over the years. In the middle ages they were burnt at the stake.

Nowadays, doctors and psychologists (the enlightened ones at least) accept homosexuality as an established fact. They don't understand why it's there but they don't try to change it. If a gay or a lesbian turns up at a clinic asking for help saying, 'I know I'm gay but I just can't cope with it, please help me, please make me straight,' their task won't be to turn that person's sexuality around but to help them accept what they really are.

Luckily there's a very good network of befriending groups for gays and lesbians and you can see details of these in the 'Contacts' section at the end of this book.

How common is it and would I recognise it?

No one knows for sure how many people are homosexual. However, researchers have produced estimates and these vary from about 1 to 10 per cent of the population. That's a pretty staggering number when you think that many people say they don't know anyone who's gay and they've never met anyone who is. The simple answer is that of course they do, and they have, it's just they haven't realised it. It's possible that there are as many bisexuals as homosexuals. Many people go through life forming relationships first with one sex and then the other. Others marry and maintain a fairly stable relationship while having a series of homosexual affairs on the side. Maybe we should consider sexuality as a wide spectrum with 100 per cent homosexuals or heterosexuals as the two extremes. Most people would probably lie somewhere in between, so that they may be aware of appreciating the attraction of their own sex even if they never choose to do anything about it.

Love and sex – what difference does being gay make?

The popular image of a gay is someone who thinks only of sex. Love and relationships don't come into it. But that's no more true than any other stereotype. Gay men and women are just as capable of long-term loving relationships as their straight counterparts. You must remember that being gay doesn't just mean an urge to have sex with someone of your own sex but feelings of romantic attraction towards that same sex.

Gays go through the same heart stopping times of 'will he ask me/won't he ask me' or 'does she love me/doesn't she love me'. Many gays and lesbians fall in love and set up home together acting very like a married couple. In fact, some research suggests that gays and lesbians are likely to have better relationships and sex lives than straight couples because they view each other on a more equal basis and their love-making is more caring and concerned with giving pleasure rather than taking it for themselves.

So that brings up the subject of sex. What do gays do? Well again, it's much the same as straight couples. They hold hands, they cuddle, they kiss. They get the same thrill down their spine when bodies 'accidentally' brush one another. They get the same urges when they start kissing and petting to go 'just that bit further'. Both gay men and lesbians make love by caressing each other and bringing each other to orgasm by mutual masturbation. It can involve oral sex and, in some cases, anal sex (see pages 65–6).

How do you know if you're gay?

The experience of realising that you're gay seems to vary from person to person. Some people I interviewed said they knew very early on, when they were a young child.

The whole situation is confused because most boys and girls have crushes on members of their own sex sometime in childhood or adolescence. This is normal and healthy and a way of developing role models; people you can look up to and try to emulate. However, many young people of both sexes get very scared at this point and think that they are homosexual when in fact they're quite likely to develop feelings for the opposite sex sooner or later.

These feelings are, of course, shared by young gays and lesbians. Discovering that you're homosexual isn't easy and because society is currently so anti-gay it can be very hard to face up to. Because of this, many homosexuals don't openly acknowledge their sexuality and don't form any sexual relationships until their mid-20s or even later.

'I had crushes on teachers at school but then we all did. Then I realised I was in love with my best friend. I wanted to get as close to her as I could but I know it made her feel uncomfortable. I used to get really embarrassed in the showers at school 'cos I wanted to look at her, and the other girls, but knew I shouldn't. No one really suspected me but I felt guilty all the time as though I had to hold myself back.'

'I always knew there was something different about me but I suppose I never really put it into words for myself until I was about 16. I didn't know anyone who was gay and I certainly didn't know anyone I could talk to about it. I searched through all the programmes on television and if there was anything that was on gays I watched it. I tried to tape them in secret so I could go over and over them again when my parents were out.'

Coming out – telling family and friends

This is the big step. You know that your family and friends may not understand but you want to tell them anyway. You want to be honest. But it isn't easy.

SNIGGERS AND GIGGLES

This is one boy's experience.

'I made the stupid mistake of telling my best friend that I was head over heels in love with him. I'd been in love with him for five years. I built up to it. I said to him months beforehand that there's something I had to tell him. I was terrified, so nervous. I finally said it, "I'm gay." It was incredibly difficult to say. I was shaking and this was the first person I'd ever said it to.

He said, "That's fine as long as you don't try anything on with me," and that's really the reaction I found with most people. I laughed it off with him and said, "I wouldn't fancy you anyway." Then we had a social studies lesson about homosexuality at school. The whole lesson was completely against homosexuality. I was just terrified about the whole thing. I came out of the lesson in tears. I was so upset. It was obvious that something was wrong.

I went home and I couldn't talk to my mum but I went to one of her friends for help. She suggested that I call up a local radio helpline. I did it but it was absolutely no use whatsoever. I couldn't believe it. I'd heard people call up before. But because I was only 15 I seemed to be completely rejected. I came off the phone worse off than when I went on.

Next I decided I had to tell my parents. I tried to tell my mum and I got my mates round to help me with it. I tried to plan it. I waited till they were watching *Brookside* and then I said, "How would you feel if you had a homosexual in the family?" My dad said it was something we'd never have to face so it didn't really matter. I said, "Well you may have to face it from now on," and walked out of the room. My mum said that I couldn't possibly know and told me to come back when I was 21 and talk about it again. I'm an only child as well so that doesn't really help things. My parents rejecting the fact that I was gay was the worst thing. They were the first people who said to me "don't be silly".

The next week I went to a party and got very drunk. The whole school found out. I didn't know what to do. One of the teachers came up and said, "We've all heard about your problem and we want you to know the staff are behind you 100 per cent." I was dead embarrassed but in a way it was nice to know that they did know.

Suddenly I found people started bringing me all their problems, trusting me, because I had a big problem myself. It had quite a good effect because I made a lot of friends and I didn't lose any of my old ones either. Everyone stuck by me. That was really fantastic.'

This boy had the sensible idea of talking to someone outside his family first; in this case a friend of his mum's. Knowing that there is an adult who accepts your homosexuality makes it easier to raise the subject at home. Unfortunately parents don't always receive the news very well. They may try to deny or reject the idea as in the above case or they can blame themselves for how you are, going back over all your childhood years wondering where they went wrong. Some parents even try to get their sons or daughters 'cured' to make them straight. This is very hard to take if you're not feeling good about yourself in the first place so, if you can, it's important to emphasise that being gay is how you are; nobody has to feel guilty about it and you yourself feel good that way. Give them time and they'll usually come round. There are also groups who will talk to parents of gay children and the 'Contacts' section at the end of the book gives some information on this.

All in all, telling people is never going to be easy and there will always be friends and relations who won't be able to come to terms with it.

Most people choose to tell a close friend first to 'test the water' but the next step isn't always obvious. This is where talking to a Helpline or contacting a Gay/Lesbian Club can come in. See the section on getting help later in this chapter and the addresses at the end of the book.

Risks

Promiscuity, whether gay or straight, carries a large risk. The more partners you have, the more likely you are to contract a whole variety of sexual diseases including AIDS. In the early years of AIDS (see Chapter 12), HIV – that's the virus that seems to cause AIDS – spread particularly fast among the male homosexual communities because anal sex often involves some tearing of tissues around the rectum and loss of blood. When semen and blood mix, the HIV virus is most easily transferred. So far there doesn't appear to be any significant degree of HIV in the lesbian community and this is probably because lesbians tend to favour 'safer' sex anyway.

You can see more information on safe sex in the chapter on HIV and AIDS but basically it means avoiding anything that involves a transfer of body fluids. These could be blood, semen, vaginal and cervical fluids and breast milk. Gay men should always wear a strong condom, preferably one that has been treated with spermicide. Look for BSI tested condoms (check for the Kite Mark on the pack) as these are the safest. Oral sex can also be risky, particularly if a woman is menstruating or the active partner has cuts or sores in his/her mouth. Using a condom or avoiding oral sex during your female partner's period is a sensible precaution.

Coming out or telling friends and colleagues is a risk in itself. The scare and panic surrounding the spread of AIDS is only making things worse so while you may wish to be honest with the world in general you may find it safer to restrict the truth to a small circle of close friends and family.

The law

In England, Scotland and Wales the age of consent for male homosexuals is 21. In other words, it is illegal to have homosexual intercourse with a man under the age of 21. This is an anomaly because the age of consent for other sexual acts is 16. Over the age of 21 homosexuality is legal for consenting adults (i.e. both partners know what they're doing and agree to it) in 'privacy'. By privacy they really mean within the four walls and a locked door. Whereas a boy and girl might receive some embarrassing comments and laughter if they were caught making love on a beach or in a park, two gays could be in big trouble.

A recent change in policy in Scotland means that male gays between the ages of 16 and 21 (and therefore technically under the homosexual age of consent) are now less likely to be prosecuted. This may be the first step in a move to bring the age of consent for gays (21) into line with that of the rest of the population (16).

Lesbianism, however, is not illegal in the UK. The story goes that when the law on homosexuality was being written in Queen Victoria's time, the Queen refused to believe that women did 'anything like that'. In other words, by royal decree, female homosexuality does not exist. And what doesn't exist cannot be either legal or illegal!

Getting help and support

There is a network of Gay Switchboards and befriending agencies throughout the country. You can get details of your local one from London Gay Switchboard on 071-837 7324 though you may have to wait quite a long time before you can get through on the phone. Alternatively, you can look in your local paper in the personal column or ring directory enquiries or look in the phone book.

Many young people who are just beginning to accept the fact that they are gay use these agencies as a first person to talk to.

I asked the secretary of one of the local befriending groups what usually happens when someone rings up.

'First of all, people often ring up, listen while we say hello, and then they hang up. It takes a lot of courage before they can actually speak. I imagine that some people ring up two, three, maybe half a dozen times before they can get a word out. That's okay, we understand how hard it is to get that first word spoken.

We try to sound as helpful as possible. We describe the youth group that we run, and we arrange to meet them before a meeting. They might call back a couple of times for reassurance. Then, and even then, about 50 per cent of them won't turn up.

I always ask callers, "Am I the first gay person you've ever spoken to?" I then usually arrange to meet them outside the meeting. I tell them a bit about myself so they'll recognise me and I wait there. Then I go up to them and say, "Are you supposed to be going to my youth group and is your name so and so?" I introduce myself. Then we go along and I introduce them round to other people. It can be sticky at a first meeting but usually I try and make sure they speak to two or three other people.

When you listen to the conversations going round in the room it's nothing about being gay. It's just people being comfortable in a group when they know that something's understood and doesn't need to be talked about. It's somewhere we can go to be ourselves. Sex doesn't even come into it all that much. It's like coming home.'

Myths about homosexuality

Homosexuals corrupt young people. No they don't. Homosexuals aren't evangelists! They don't try and recruit for the cause. Most gays and lesbians are only too aware that they're out on a limb with their sexuality. Even if they fancy someone who's straight the last thing they want is the antagonism and the pain of rejection that comes from propositioning someone who isn't interested and who may be even disgusted by the proposal.

Lesbians are women trying to be men. No they aren't. Many people think of lesbians as butch, aggressive, masculine type women.

Again, there are a few, usually the ones who hit the headlines, who are highly aggressive and tend to adopt male personalities. The rise of feminism and the fearful reaction that it has brought about in many people has strengthened this view. But not all feminists are lesbians. And not all lesbians are feminists.

Gays and lesbians really want to change their sex. No they don't. This is wrong. A gay wants to be a man loved by other men and a lesbian wants to be a woman loved by other women. There are some people who are convinced that they are 'trapped inside a body of the wrong sex' and some of these do live successfully as a member of the opposite sex without anyone knowing. These people are called transsexuals but they have very little to do with homosexuality.

Homosexuals fancy young boys. No they don't. Many people think that homosexuals are just waiting to pounce on young, good-looking boys. This is not true. Most crimes against young boys, or young girls, are carried out by people with severe emotional problems to whom youth, innocence or lack of power is the turn-on, *not* homosexuality.

CHAPTER FOUR

A first date

In fairy stories and romances the hero meets the heroine's eyes across a crowded room. They glide together, as if by magic. The violins throb higher and higher. Their hands touch and electricity fills the air. Romance has triumphed.

Real life isn't always so straightforward. For a start, you know, and I know, that often there is no such thing as 'a first date'. Usually you meet someone you like the look of at a disco, club or party. You chat a bit and give them the eye. The next move is when the bloke (and it still usually is the bloke) says, 'See you next week then.' Is it a date? Have you been asked out? Or does he really mean, 'Well that was a right waste of an evening, next time you won't see me for dust.'

If that happens to you, you've got two obvious choices. You can either wait until the next week and see if he turns up (and if he does, whether he takes any interest in you) or you can take a deep breath and say, 'Is that a date? Are you asking me out?' At least that way you'll know.

Asking someone out

The real reason that people find it so difficult to ask someone out is the fear of rejection.

So let's imagine that there is someone you have seen around who you like the look of. They probably know you by sight and they may have smiled and been friendly but there is nothing more than that. What do you do?

If you have mutual friends you can use a go-between. Personally, I don't think that is always a very good idea. You can never be sure what the intermediary is actually saying and you only have their word for it what the reaction was.

No, if you want to ask someone out the best person to do it is you. After all, the worst that can happen is that they say no ... well, that is not exactly true because I suppose the real worst thing would be if they and their friends all laughed about it in front of you. For that reason I suggest that you try not to do it in front of too many other people.

Some boys say they would be delighted to be asked out by a girl because then they'd start off on the right foot knowing that the girl was really interested but others said they might be a bit put off by a girl taking such an assertive role. If you're a girl in this position, one good way of hedging your bets is to ask the boy to join in some group activity that you or someone else has organised e.g. you're all going off to the fair, or to help at the old people's home or to suss out the new leisure centre etc. If you make the invitation friendly and casual sounding it allows you to make the first move and leaves them to show how interested or not they may be.

There is also the old line of 'I just happened to have these two tickets . . .' It may be corny but it still works. You say that you've been given these two tickets to a concert or a film or something and that your friend has let you down at the last moment. You're looking for someone who might be interested in seeing it with you and would they like to come? That way the issue is whether or not they want to see the show – not whether or not they want to be with you. It usually comes to the same thing in the end but it allows them to feel less pressured and also to back out more gracefully if they're not interested. The pay off is that quite often even if the boy doesn't accept your invitation he will think about it for a week or so and then ask you out instead.

Being asked out

If you get asked out and you want to go then that's easy. You just say yes. If you would like to go out with them but you can't get to whatever it is they are suggesting or you don't like the idea of it then you should say so. Suggest something that you would like to do instead. The problem comes when you don't want to go out with them.

Refusal and rejection is not easy to take. So if you have got to laugh, at least wait until they're out of sight. And it doesn't really do any harm to be polite, does it? If someone asks you out, you can at least say thanks but no thanks. 'You must be joking' destroys their morale and makes you sound like a pompous prat.

Where do you go?

'Oh, the cinema's favourite if you don't know the girl. You don't have to talk so much and then when you come out you've got something to talk about.'

'It's nice going out on a Saturday afternoon rather than just in the evening. Into town maybe. Going somewhere together and doing something, something that you can talk about.'

If you are asking someone out for the first time, it's always a good idea to have something in mind when you offer the invitation. It's all very well saying, 'Would you like to come out and what would you like to do?' but most people even if they wanted to accept, wouldn't be able to come up with any brilliant ideas off the top of their head. So plan something first. It's the planning that is important, not the magnitude of what you have to offer.

One word of warning here particularly to boys. However self-confident the girl may appear to you, she is almost certainly going to be nervous on a first date (more about this in a minute) and to some extent she may even be scared of you. Don't make things worse by trying to manoeuvre her into a corner or enclosed space with you.

As one girl said:

'I once got asked out by this bloke next door who's really nice. He was 17 and he could drive. I was only 15. He said he'd borrow his brother's car and take me out but I wouldn't go because I was scared. I think I just didn't know what would be expected of me. I didn't want to be in that car with him.'

The art of self presentation (i.e. looking your best)

There are two good reasons for making a special effort about your general appearance when you go out with someone; it makes you feel better about yourself and it's a compliment to your date.

Cleanliness

Everyone has got their own style of hair, make-up, clothes etc, and I'm not for one minute suggesting that you should change that style in the hope of pleasing someone you hardly know. What matters is what's underneath. And I don't mean the clean underwear just in case you get knocked down and have to go to hospital, I mean YOU. You don't have to smother yourself in perfumes and aftershaves and deodorants, just make sure you're clean. Brush your teeth at the last minute. Scrub your finger nails. Even if they're bitten, clean ragged stumps look better than dirty ones. Scruffy holey jeans are fine. Scruffy holey smelly ones aren't.

'Whether or not I go out with someone depends on their appearance. You just look at some of them and think—"no way, not ever".'

'They've got to be clean. No greasy hair or dirty fingernails. I mean how can anyone not have a bath before going out on a Saturday night? All the girls make an effort so why shouldn't they?

Clothes

Wear something that makes you feel good.

Girls in particular can be inclined to over dress. It's nice to look special and you are paying them a great compliment by taking the trouble but some boys can be scared and put off if you turn up at McDonald's dressed like you are expecting to go to a ritzy club.

Nerves

Everyone gets nervous before a first date. There's not a whole lot you can do about nerves apart from trying to hang on to the belief that you will survive and however bad you feel, you're not likely to make as much of a prat of yourself as you think. If you come over very wobbly a few deep breaths of fresh air and a glass of cold water can help. Three vodka and tonics probably won't.

'I've even asked a girl out and gone to pick her up at her house and turned back at the gate. Not because I didn't want to see her but because I was just too scared. I really liked her but I couldn't explain what happened.'

'My family all make fun of me because I shut myself in the bathroom for so long before I go out. They think I'm tarting myself up but actually I'm on the loo. My insides just turn to water.'

What do you talk about?

Everyone has experienced the Big Silence. They are not saying anything, you can't think of anything to say and you're both surreptitiously trying to look at your watch. It doesn't have to be like that.

It's another old Agony Aunt's saying, but most people's favourite topic of conversation is themselves. So give them an opportunity to talk about themselves. It's also a good way of getting over your feelings of shyness. If you try to sound genuinely interested in someone, it diverts the spotlight from you and you'll quickly find that you actually are interested in them. Think of a few simple questions before you go out together. 'What did you think of . . . ? Did you see . . . ?' Try to avoid questions that can be answered with a simple yes or no. It doesn't matter so much what you ask or what they say, it's just important to get them talking and for you to be able to look interested. The more you can chat, the more relaxed you will be together. And the more relaxed and comfortable you become, the less the odd empty silence will matter.

How far do you go?

This one is up to you. The most important thing is that you never do anything because you feel that it is expected of you or because you feel you owe it as a reward to someone for taking you out.

From the young people I spoke to, it seemed that the younger the boy the further he expected, or at least hoped, the girl would go on the first date. Some of them were quite honest that they were out for what they could get. They were also honest enough to admit that they were more likely to ask a girl out again if they didn't get very far with her. If they got the impression that a girl was 'easy' they would start to think that she was probably like that with other blokes too and most boys don't want to risk their reputation by going out with someone their friends might call a slag.

Will I ever see you again?

Quite often there is a moment of panic that strikes as the evening draws to a close. You've enjoyed yourself, but have they? Do they really like you? Do they really want to see you again? Try to remember that you're both probably wondering exactly the same thing.

The best way to put both of you out of your misery is for one of you to suggest another meeting. It doesn't matter which one of you does it. Just try not to make it sound as though your life depended on it.

If the evening hasn't been a raving success, and quite frankly you would rather have stayed at home with *EastEnders* and an old movie, it still won't hurt you to say thank you. If pressed you can always agree to a second date and then phone or write to cancel it. But if you are going to do that, do it quickly. Standing someone up is a coward's way out.

A word of warning on the subject of safety

I wish it wasn't necessary to say this, but there are a few cases every so often of girls going out on dates and never coming back. The chances are that you are going to go out with someone you know or your friends know but you should always tell someone who it is you are meeting and where you are going (if you know in advance). It doesn't have to be your mum, you can tell your best friend if you like, but if anything did happen, whether it was an attack or a car crash or some other kind of disaster, that piece of information could save everyone a lot of worry.

Also, and I hope this is obvious, if you are a girl going out with someone for the first time who you don't know well, try to go somewhere where there are other people. Babysitting in a friend's house or drives out into the country can be dangerous. Be sensible. And don't assume it could never happen to you.

CHAPTER FIVE

Breaking up

There's an old song that says 'breaking up is so very hard to do' but in fact it's something that most of us end up having a good deal of practice in. Statistically, it's very unlikely that you will spend the rest of your life with your first girl or boyfriend. If you are deep in the throes of your first love affair then that's the last thing you want to hear just now but you can always choose to skip this next bit and reassure yourself that you are one of the few, very few, whose first love is going to last for ever.

So if most people go through more than one relationship it follows that they also have a series of break-ups. Rule 1 here is, whichever side you're on and however it happens, breaking up *is* very hard to do.

'I just don't know how to put someone down nicely. I usually end up doing it over the phone so that I don't have to look at their face.'

'It's the worst thing that ever happened to me. I couldn't stop shaking and I had to rush to the loo in the pub and throw up. All I could think was "But why can't you love me?"'

If you are on the receiving end

Being ditched or chucked by someone you care for is one of the most difficult things you may ever have to face. The very fact that you love them means that you are likely to take their point of view as the only valid point of view in the world. So if they suddenly turn around and say, 'I don't want you any more,' where does that leave you? If they are saying that they find you boring or worthless or just not good enough, do you have to accept their judgement? Should you give up all hope of finding someone to share your life?

Certainly it's very hard not to, particularly if it all comes out of

BREAKING UP

the blue. Even if you've been half expecting it you still get that awful, stomach-lurching, sick feeling when your partner says, 'Look, there's something I think I ought to tell you . . .'

So how are you supposed to cope? Well, in the first place don't be afraid to feel all the emotions that are washing over you. You may think you are going to throw up. You may start shaking and feel freezing, even on a summer's day.

Half of you is saying, 'This can't be happening' and the other half knows only too well that it is.

These are all normal reactions to shock. It's similar to the way you would feel if someone close to you died. And, in a way, it is death. It's a death of your relationship. As with any death, you have to allow yourself time to grieve.

Grieving involves depression and this shows up in different ways. Some people stuff themselves stupid and others go on semi-hunger strikes. I know when I'm depressed I start sleeping for hours as though my mind was trying to switch off from real life.

People tend to think that it's wrong to go round telling your friends how awful you feel and if you go on doing it for months on end they are likely to get pretty sick of you. But there's nothing wrong in having a good old wallow in your grief. That's where a close friend or a brother or sister or even a mum comes in particularly handy. Get any old photos you've got of the two of you, all the gifts that you were given, and all the other souvenirs you've got in that drawer. Remember the good times and have a really good howl. This sort of crying can be good for both boys and girls.

After a bit, you'll feel some anger creeping in along with the sorrow. 'How dare he do this to me?' 'Who does she think she is?' 'I'm not going to spend the rest of my life miserable just because you were too stupid to recognise a good thing when you saw it.' Feel that anger and harness it because it's going to give you the energy to get through the next few days, weeks or even months.

You're going to use the experience to make yourself stronger and you're going to show everyone (and particularly your ex-love) that you can survive.

Should I try to get him/her back?

Don't make the mistake of going running after them. When someone says it's over, they either know what they're talking about and really mean it or they're playing some nasty little game of their own that involves you being a fish on a hook that's allowed to wriggle away a bit and then gets pulled back in, particularly grateful to feel the hook tug on your mouth again. Either way, it's time to do a Dick Whittington, pack your red-spotted handkerchief and leave.

Pathetic telephone calls and sad little letters aren't going to mend things (or not for long, anyway). And acting like a bewildered dog who'll do anything, just anything, to please its owner if the owner would just say the word, isn't going to help either. Dignity and pride may seem like old-fashioned qualities but they can be surprisingly comforting in times like these. Don't chuck them away needlessly.

How can I ever forget him/her?

The short answer is, you can't. But eventually the memories will fade and blend in with the rest of your life and you'll stop holding your breath every time the phone rings. Of course, this takes time, and it takes even longer if you torture yourself needlessly. So, for a start, you should now chuck away all your mementos. Or at least you should pack them out of sight, sealed up in an old shoe box. Once you've had your first wild orgy of wailing and grieving, put all the bits and pieces away and concentrate on getting on with life. It'll seem like a hard performance at first but eventually you'll find that you don't have to act any more.

'I thought I'd never get over him. The worst bit was when I'd managed to stop thinking about him all day and even started going out with other boys. I thought, "Great, it's over" and then the dreams started. I'd dream it was all a mistake and we were back together. Every morning I'd wake up crying. How can you ever hope to feel better when your subconscious plays lousy tricks like that on you? But somehow you do.'

Make a fuss of yourself. Tell yourself that you are convalescing after a long illness and try to come up with things that will help the patient (i.e. you) feel excited about life again. Try to think of things that you've always wanted to do and now spend the time doing them. Arrange to go and see that old school friend of yours who moved away. Have your hair highlighted. Get together with your mates and organise a really great girls' (or boys') night out.

The rebound trap

One word of warning here. Some people do meet the new partner of their dreams the day after they break up but many more push themselves into a new relationship just to '*show them*'. '*Them*', in this case, can be friends and bystanders or the ex-partner. It's a wonderfully spiteful feeling to be able to say, 'Yah boo sucks. Look what (or rather who) I've got.' But the feeling soon wears off and you can be left holding hands with someone who, in a saner moment, you wouldn't have touched with a barge pole.

Well-meaning friends often make things worse here. They want to fix you up because, apart from feeling sorry for you, having you moping around on your own makes them uncomfortable. There's no harm in meeting new people but it's generally best to give yourself time to grieve for one love affair before starting the next.

What if you're the one that wants to end the relationship?

A spot of tact and diplomacy won't cost you anything though there's no need to go over the top. Nowadays no one's going to believe, 'My darling, you are just too good for me. I cannot live up to you and so must say farewell.' But 'Well I met this girl at the disco and she's got bigger tits than you,' isn't going to go down too well either.

Remember that one of the worst things about being chucked is that it leaves you feeling rejected and worthless. So try to soften the rejection and give the person some sense of value. Even if you've been screwing up your courage for weeks to do the chucking and every word they say now irritates you, you can still pad it all out with phrases like 'I've really enjoyed some of our times together. I'll never forget you, I'm sorry I really don't want to hurt you, it's nobody's fault, it's just things aren't working out between us,' etc. etc.

'The worst thing is when they ask you "why" and you just can't tell them. Usually you have to end up making up reasons like pressure of work or family problems. They don't believe you but they can't really argue.'

If at all possible, try and tell them face to face. At the very least write a short letter and then give them a chance to see you so that you can get your goodbyes over and done with.

Leaving someone to find out for themselves or hear it from one of their mates is a real coward's way out. And it'll cause you more trouble in the long run because when that happens you are much more likely to get the endless phone calls, the requests for help with school work and, even worse, the 'I was just passing so I thought I'd call in and see if you were busy' line.

What happens if you've told them it's over and they won't let go?

You've got to be firm.

Some people can't accept that a relationship has finished and so they keep on phoning, writing or turning up on your doorstep. They are desperately searching for the slightest sign that you still care. Any response you make – even if it's only a few friendly words – will be taken as confirmation that everything's okay again.

If you get stuck in this position, say that you don't want to hurt them any more than you already have, so you are not going to see or talk to them for a while. And then make sure that you don't.

Can ex-lovers become 'just good friends'?

Yes, they can but it does take a bit of time for readjustment. There nearly always has to be a period after the break-up when they avoid each other and work through their feelings of disappointment, guilt or whatever. Some people are never able to make the change but others seem to thrive on the friendships that develop out of old loves.

'One of my best mates now is an old boyfriend. I suppose it helped that we were friends long before we went out together. It was difficult at first when we split up and, even tho' I finished things, I still felt a bit choked when I first saw him with another girl. But after a while we found it easier to see each other and now we muck around a lot together but it's as friends, not lovers.'

CHAPTER SIX

Staying together

I suppose one definition of staying together, going steady or being an item is when you start to plan ahead with your partner. For girls, you are still excited and pleased every time he rings you but you are expecting that phone call, not just hoping for it. For boys there is the relief of knowing you don't have to go out and impress someone in the hope they'll go out with you – because they already are! And you both realise that even if life trips you up in some way, there's one person who's always going to be on your side.

The advantages

It can make a vast difference to your self-confidence.

It gives you a chance to get very close to someone outside of your own family. Some girls, and boys, talk more honestly to their partners than they've ever been able to do with their own mates. And their partners listen sympathetically.

With a bit of luck, it allows you to relax enough for your own personality to reveal itself. In other words, you don't have to be on best behaviour with each other all the time. Learning that someone (apart from your mum) will still love you despite your moods and ups and downs is very important. And so is learning to love someone else through theirs!

The disadvantages

It takes up a lot of time! If you were suffering from terminal boredom before you met them you might be glad of this but it can make it very difficult to fit in schoolwork, hobbies, family obligations and just seeing other friends.

STAYING TOGETHER

And because of this, if you're not careful, you can find yourself losing friends or at least drifting away from them.

It's natural to want to be like your loved one and admire what they admire but, if you're not careful, you can find yourself turning into a carbon copy. It's usually other people, particularly your family, who'll draw your attention to this. If you find that your likes and dislikes with regard to music, fashion, clubs etc, change drastically with each new partner then perhaps you ought to ask yourself whether you're being a bit too much of a chameleon for your own personality ever to be seen.

How do you fit it in with family and friends?

The answer to this is – with great difficulty. Be prepared to be teased. There's always the aunties who want to coo 'our Johnny's got a girlfriend'. Just grit your teeth and give them a sickening smile.

And however inseparable the two of you are, do try to understand that there are times when your family would like to see you on your own.

Coping with your friends' reaction can be more problematical. We owe friends our loyalty and though no one's suggesting you should always take along a gooseberry when you go out together, you ought to make an effort to have the occasional girls' or lads' night out. And if you're caught on the other end of this, i.e. all your friends have got themselves partners and you're left on your own, then try to be brave and honest enough to say to them, 'Look, I miss you, don't I deserve some friendship too? How about a night off from him/her every so often so we can do something together?' If you're feeling abandoned by your friends try to understand that it isn't usually a case of wilful neglect but more of absentmindedness in the face of love. A little reminder can work wonders.

What if your parents don't approve?

It may be that your parents wouldn't approve of anyone or it could be that there's something particular about him or her that they don't like. It's difficult to sort this out and it leads to endless rows and atmospheres at home. However, if your relationship's going to be long running it's often better to try to sort this out rather than ignore it and carry on seeing each other against your parents' wishes.

If your parents don't like your boyfriend then you should ask them why. If they've got a good reason listen to it and then try to present your side of things. Rather than avoiding them, make a point of inviting him round when they're there so they can see how nice he is for themselves. The thing that will influence them most is if they see him treating you with love and respect.

It's probably worth saying something here about coping with parental disapproval. Next time you have a disagreement over something, e.g. your girl or boyfriend, don't shout demands and stamp about showing off your temper. Sit down and act very cool and try to discuss your differences. If they start shouting ask them if they can sit down and talk things over reasonably with you. This is usually such a shock to parents that they'll comply. And it can work wonders. If you both try to listen carefully to the other's argument you can nearly always negotiate some kind of compromise. Try it and see.

Jealousy and freedom

How much freedom should you give each other if you're going steady? Well, that usually depends on the balance between trust and jealousy in your relationship. Some people *are* very jealous. It may be because they've had a bad experience in the past making them feel insecure or it could just be part of their personality. But it's very difficult to deal with. If you have a jealous partner you can find yourself running in ever decreasing circles trying to prove to them that everything's okay. So it's important to understand that jealousy is a highly destructive emotion and that it can only really be controlled by the person who feels jealous. And if they can't get to grips with controlling it, then the rest of their life could be pretty miserable.

If you know that you're severely jealous and that this doesn't actually have much foundation in the relationship i.e. your partner isn't going off with other people all the time it's just that you're scared that they might, then it's probably a good idea to consider having some counselling. See the 'Contacts' section for suggestions. Talking things over with an experienced counsellor will help you feel more secure in yourself and in turn this will dramatically improve your relationship.

Rows and making up

Your way of coping with anger depends very much on how your family copes with it – either bottling up or sulking, or letting all hell rip loose.

On the whole, most couples do have rows. They may be about silly things or major issues. Either way, there are several important things to remember. First of all, there are times when you will just have to agree to disagree. Some arguments can't be resolved and, short of continuing the row for days or weeks on end, you just have to accept that you have different attitudes. You can either negotiate a compromise or avoid the danger area. Secondly, if you've had a row, and the atmosphere is rather frosty, never be afraid to take the first step to try to get things back on a warmer footing. You may feel that it wasn't your fault and that you're giving in by reaching out to the other person. If you love each other, fault is irrelevant. Don't think 'it's not my turn to give in' just reach out and say 'let's be friends'. This doesn't mean that you're admitting that their attitude was right and yours was wrong. It's just acknowledging that your feelings for each other are more important than the disagreement.

Finally, here's a piece of advice for anyone who has a partner who sulks. This can be hellishly difficult to cope with because anything you say is bound to be wrong. I think your best bet is to wait until things are more or less back to normal (and it usually does happen eventually), catch them in a good mood and then say, 'Look, I just want to ask you this because I think it would help me a lot if I knew. When you get upset and you go sort of sulky, how do you advise me to cope with you? Should I leave you alone or jolly you up or what?' Strangely enough, most people know how they want to be treated when they feel upset and angry and if you ask them they'll tell you. And it does help.

Responsibilities

One of my interviewees said that going steady involves honesty, fidelity and trust. I think that just about sums it up.

There is also a responsibility to protect each other. This means both emotional and physical protection. You give each other emotional support simply by being there. Couples in a good relationship don't try and score points off each other or put the other down. It's not that they're never critical, it's just that they try to give criticism in a positive way.

Protecting each other physically doesn't just mean walking your girlfriend to her door on a dark night; it also implies using your common sense about health and sex. I sometimes get letters from girls who are scared they might be pregnant but who have never done anything about contraception because they're 'too embarrassed' to talk to their boyfriends about it. As I keep saying, sex is an adult activity and if you're not ready to take responsibility for what you're doing then you've no business to be having sex.

Long-distance relationships – can they survive?

Some people seem to choose long-distance relationships, but others have no choice in the matter. People move, go away to college, start a new job somewhere else.

This kind of relationship requires a great deal of faith and trust.

It's not realistic to expect someone that you're not going to see for weeks to stay at home every night labelling their stamp collection. They, and you, should be able to enjoy a good social life in between the glorious occasions when you're together. That includes parties and discos and clubs and in most cases it's not surprising that you're likely to meet up with a lot of temptation. It does require dedication to carry on going out with someone who isn't there!

However I suspect that more long-distance relationships falter when the long-distance part itself is removed. Say your boy or girlfriend is away at college. The summer vacation starts and you've got three months together. If all the time you've ever had together was a week at most, every one of your meetings will have been charged with the excitement of meeting and with the sadness of parting. When you see each other day in, day out, that can quickly go missing and things can become very flat. It's also very strange how people who can be so loving and caring in their letters and phone calls just turn into ordinary mortals when you sit face to face, or side by side in conversation.

So if you are considering committing yourself to this kind of relationship, try to think hard and sort out the realities from your fantasies.

The temptation to make it permanent

When you've been going out together for a while it's only natural to wonder 'what next?'. The obvious answer (though sometimes it's more obvious to one partner than the other!) is to get engaged, but I think it's often a mistake and can even be a sign of desperation. If you are right for one another then you'll enjoy being together and your relationship will progress at its own rate. But if you're scared about losing your partner or worried about what he or she is doing when they're out of your sight it can be awfully tempting to get engaged so that everyone knows they 'belong' to you.

Friends and family can push you in this direction too. Mums and aunties are prone to ask coy questions about when they're going to hear the wedding bells and you may find yourself getting carried away with the idea before you've had a chance to think through the real implications.

Getting engaged

Big engagement parties can make you feel very important and everyone will be pleased and excited for you. But it also makes your relationship very public. Any slip or quarrel will be remarked upon and quite soon you'll find your family taking bets as to whether you'll make it to the wedding or not. Being engaged gives a nice pleasant feeling of security but some people start thinking they own each other. Whereas last week it may have been okay for you to go off for an evening with your friends, this week, now you're engaged, it causes a major row. And if the worst does happen and you split up, the split also becomes a public spectacle. You either have to inform everyone who knows you that you've broken up or go through months of meeting people in the street who ask you how the wedding plans are going.

What if one partner is pressing for a commitment?

Sometimes one member of the couple is extremely keen to get engaged. A typical example of this is the girlfriend who constantly walks her boyfriend backwards and forwards in front of jewellers' shops. She drops hints at every birthday and Christmas and waves her left hand around in the air imagining a large diamond twinkling on her third finger. But sometimes it's the boy who wants the commitment. He wants to be able to label the girl as his and have everyone know that she belongs to him and no one else. If that's what you both want then fine. But neither of you should be pushed into it unless you're completely sure. Remember what I said earlier about jealousy and insecurity? If your partner suffers from these, don't think it's going to make them any better just because you're wearing their ring. It'll work for a while but then the old nagging worries will start.

In this case, it's much better, and kinder, to be honest. Tell them how fond you are of them and reassure them that you want to continue with them but that you just don't feel able to commit yourself to engagement and marriage. And remember, it's much better to get this out in the open and actually say it than make excuses, half promises and generally lead them on just for the sake of a quiet life.

CHAPTER SEVEN

Approaching sex

'It's time you knew the facts of life'

Some parents are horribly aware of their duty to tell their offspring 'the facts of life'. Other parents never quite seem to get round to talking about it at all. They worry about it a lot, of course, and every so often they ask you what you're doing in biology in school. But their eventual pearls of wisdom usually boil down to 'don't play with yourself and if you're going to do *it* for heaven's sake make sure she's on the Pill' in the case of a boy and 'Here's some sanitary towels and make sure you don't get into trouble' in the case of girls. All in all, there are likely to be a few gaps in the information you receive about sex. The physical part, with particular emphasis on intercourse, will probably sound straightforward but lots of people are left completely in the dark about the emotional side to sex.

Sex raises its ugly head

Major changes take place in the body during puberty. Around this time both boys and girls become highly aware of their own sexuality and their own capacity for sexual arousal. It seems that more boys than girls masturbate and they also start doing it earlier. There are probably several reasons for this. The hormones responsible for sexual arousal seem to be more concentrated in boys and they become aroused 'from cold' more easily. But the biggest difference of all is that a boy's sexual parts are far more obvious to him and the rest of the world than those of a girl. Because his penis and testicles hang outside his body they get rubbed and jostled and therefore excited by everyday life. It's not surprising that he quickly discovers the right way to touch them to bring about the most pleasure.

Masturbation often carries a large burden of guilt. Most people know nowadays that it doesn't make you go blind or your hair fall out but they still feel that they shouldn't really be doing it. Some of them regard it as a sign that they're 'giving in' to their body's urges and others just think that it's dirty and wrong. In fact, it's a very healthy and normal thing and a safe way of relieving sexual tensions. Masturbation allows you to explore your body's potential for sexual arousal without hurting yourself or involving anyone else. When boys masturbate they usually carry on until they ejaculate. That means that they reach their climax or orgasm and then the penis goes into a kind of involuntary spasm and pushes out a small quantity of semen, a white sticky liquid containing sperm.

Girls are more likely to start playing with themselves because it just feels nice, warm and comforting. They know they feel excited but they don't always realise that if they go on doing it they eventually reach an orgasm. Sometimes it's a big surprise to them when it does happen.

Most young people are aware that they start having sexy thoughts and getting turned on by fantasies or day-dreams. Sometimes people are worried that they're becoming obsessed by sex. I get lots of letters saying, 'This can't be right, it's all I can think about, I'm sure there's something wrong with me, I'm going to turn into a nymphomaniac or a pervert.' The chances are that there's nothing wrong or unusual about them at all. They're just discovering how powerful and intoxicating an influence sex can be.

The ultimate cocktail

Suddenly, either after a long campaign of planning and plotting, or almost out of thin air, comes the first real sexual contact. Maybe it's just a kiss or it could be that it goes further and deeper. Tongues entwine and hands fondle breasts. WOW! Most people never forget that first feeling. Their whole body becomes supersensitive and they go home replaying in their minds the sensation of her kiss on the ear lobe and his touch on the nape of the neck. It's easy to dismiss kissing and touching as 'kid's stuff' but with the right person it becomes a mind-blowing sexual experience. Out of the blue you've been presented with the 'ultimate cocktail'. It's forbidden, naughty, dangerous and it feels wonderful. That's sex. And that is the real danger of sex. It can carry you away far beyond your normal, sane and rational judgement.

The dangers of sex

At its best, sex is an expression of love. At its worst, sex can pull you blindly into a relationship with a type of person you'd never normally give the time of day to. I get letters like these every week:

'My friends all tell me that I'm mad and crazy. They say I should leave him. He gets so angry sometimes and even hits me and beats me up. I know you'll tell me I'm being silly but I can't help it because I love him. And I know that he loves me and he needs me and that we have to be together.'

'She knows how I feel and she says she loves me but then we go out somewhere and she gets off with someone else in front of me. Sometimes she even goes home with them. She says what does it matter as long as she comes back to me. I know she's right but I just can't help being jealous. If only I could stop feeling like this everything would be okay. But as it is, every time she looks at someone else I want to kill myself.'

These are both examples of destructive relationships where one person is being badly hurt, physically or emotionally, because they aren't able to stand back and see what's going on. Nothing short of a miracle is going to get them free because the dark side of love has sunk its fangs into them.

Some people do get hooked on sex. They feel it gives them power, makes them important or just feel loved. The idea of 'a relationship' goes out of the window. They just want sex. Unfortunately they often get other things too. Like sexually transmitted diseases and even AIDS. And they lose the respect of their friends.

For girls of course there's always the added danger that they can get pregnant. 'Being careful', i.e. the boy takes his penis out before he reaches orgasm, is the most widely used form of birth control amongst teenagers today. It is notoriously unreliable and plays a major part in contributing to the 200,000 or so unplanned teenage pregnancies in Britain every year.

How to handle sex and live to tell the tale

So if sex is such a powerful force how can it be handled? Well, mainly by accepting responsibility for what you're doing and developing an awareness about your own susceptibility. For example, how influenced are you by crowds? When everyone disappears off upstairs at a party are you going to feel that you have to do it too? How likely are you to get drunk? What are you like when you're drunk? If drugs are on offer, will you take them? How susceptible are you to emotional blackmail? Do the words 'but if you really loved me you'd do it' make you jump into bed?

Develop your own set of rules. They may change with time and experience but at any one time you should know what you're prepared to do and what you're not. Remember that drink and drugs both lower your inhibitions so you're more likely to do things or go further than you would in the cold light of day, but unless you're totally paralytic or stoned out of your head (in which case sex may be the last thing on your mind) you should still be aware of your own personal warning bell sounding when you step over your limits. The trick is to listen to the bell and not shut it off, telling yourself that you couldn't help it. If you're going to do something or have sex with someone make sure it's because it's what you choose, not just because it was easier than saying no when you'd had one too many.

Stick to your rules – breaking them could leave you very unhappy, and your partner should have enough respect for you not to push you against your will. Remember that going to bed with someone isn't the next step after kissing. Two people in love can share and enjoy their sexuality just as much by kissing and cuddling as by full-scale intercourse. Kissing and petting may not seem as grown-up or exciting as intercourse, but it's still a lot of fun (if it isn't then you aren't doing it properly – or, at least, not with the right person!) and many couples choose to stick to it for a long time.

Discuss it with your girlfriend or boyfriend. What do you mean you can't talk about things like that? Sex is one of the sexiest things you can talk about. But talking about sex isn't just a come on. It can also be a way of showing and sharing your responsibility.

Sex and the law

In England, Scotland and Wales, it is an offence for any male to have sex with a girl under the age of 16. Sixteen is known as the 'age of consent' because the law considers that a girl younger than this is unable to give a fully informed and therefore properly thought out and considered answer as to whether she's willing to have sex. The age of consent is 17 in Northern Ireland and 18 in the Republic of Ireland. The age varies in other countries, and it's a good idea to be familiar with your local laws!

In England, Scotland and Wales, if the boy is over 17 then he can be prosecuted and get up to two years in prison. If the girl that he has sex with is very young i.e. under 13, then his offence is

APPROACHING SEX

considered to be extremely serious and technically he could receive life imprisonment (25 years). If the boy is under 17 then he can't be prosecuted but he could be placed in care. In order for a prosecution to take place someone, usually the girl's parents, has to report what's happened to the police. Quite often the police decide not to act but even if it never goes to court the whole business can be very frightening and upsetting.

The law is much less strict the other way round! At present, in the UK, women cannot be accused of 'unlawful sexual intercourse' but may be charged with indecent assault if they sleep with a boy who is under 16. Again, charges are rarely brought but it is as well to bear it in mind, because many women are attracted to younger boys and the reverse is also true. To a 14- or 15-year-old boy, an older teenager or woman may seem to offer the sexual excitement and experience that isn't available from his own age group.

Of course, the idea of having an age of consent is artificial. No one can seriously believe that a girl who is 15 and 364 days old is a child and 24 hours later she's an adult and knows all about sex. It is a legal device intended to provide protection for young girls. And, of course, many thousands of girls under the age of 16 do have sex. Some of them probably are taken advantage of by their boyfriends but others are actively looking for sex. Many people think that the age of consent should be lowered or even abolished.

I happen to believe that the age of consent is important. Some girls probably are ready to have sex before then but I think that most girls and boys are not mature enough emotionally until round about 16. Many of you, reading this, will disagree strongly and probably say that I don't know what I'm talking about. But you don't read the hundreds of letters I receive every month from girls as young as 12 who think that they're pregnant, or they've got AIDS, or they're desolate because their boyfriend's left them even though they've slept with him or who simply ask 'But what's all the fuss about, I've had sex, he enjoyed it but I was just left feeling nothing.' I also get letters from boys who care deeply for their girlfriends but who are horrified to discover that what was a loving sexual relationship has now turned into a pregnancy and a threat to both their futures.

Having sex isn't difficult. It can mean nothing more than a penis going inside a vagina and it can be over in as little as 10 or 15 seconds. Making love is something else. That implies a relationship, caring, trust and mutual responsibility for what you're doing with your body.

Making love should be something that you both decide to do and look forward to and learn to do together. As I said, anyone can have sex, but it takes time and patience and dedication to find out what your partner enjoys and show them and help them to learn what you like. The act of intercourse is only a minor part of making love. The exploration of each other's bodies and minds takes longer, is more important and, ultimately, gives more pleasure.

Finally, back to the question of responsibility. I consider making love to be essentially an adult activity. And if you're going to do it you have to prove that you are an adult by taking adult responsibilities for your actions. That means protecting yourself and your partner. Not just protection from pregnancy but from emotional disturbance as well. In other words, sex plays its part in a stable relationship where it adds to something that's already in existence. The opposite, the quick thrill behind the bike shed, can feel exciting and give great physical pleasure, mainly to the boy, but leaves nothing behind it. If there's no basic relationship sex leaves you with the taste of ashes. It disturbs you and leaves you feeling unsatisfied and looking for something else.

If you sleep with each other or even if you think there's a possibility it might happen, you must talk about birth control first. It doesn't matter who brings the topic up and it doesn't make any difference if neither of you is the world's great expert on different methods. Some girls think that talking about birth control makes them sound as though they've been around a lot while they would prefer to look innocent. This is one game where innocence equals stupidity! If neither of you are very sure about birth control then you can always go along together to a family planning clinic. Have a look at the chapter on contraception for more information about this. Remember that a boy who takes the trouble to get involved with this side of things and accompany his girlfriend to a doctor, is showing how much he cares. Sometimes though, people don't get it together to visit a clinic before they make love for the first time and in that instance a boy can show how much he cares by wearing

APPROACHING SEX

a sheath. Saying they feel funny or it's not natural is just downright stupid. If your boyfriend tries that line on just tell him that it's not him who's going to get pregnant.

So what I'm trying to say, really, is UNLESS YOU'RE READY AND ABLE TO TAKE RESPONSIBILITY FOR WHAT YOU'RE DOING, YOU'RE NOT READY TO HAVE SEX.

CHAPTER EIGHT

Sex – the mechanics and the fun

Girls – the outside

The main difference between a teenage girl and a teenage boy is that the girl goes in and out a lot more having (to a greater or lesser extent) curvy breasts, a narrower waist and curvier hips and bottom. And, of course, she doesn't have a penis.

A girl is usually particularly aware of her breasts, often because it's the size, or lack of size, of them that boys comment on most. Breasts obviously are attractive to men but not all men lust after enormous boobs. (You can see more about breast worries in the chapter on Sexual Health.)

Between the girl's legs there are three openings into the body. Starting at the front, there's a very small opening called the urethra and it's out of here that the urine flows. The middle opening is the vagina or sexual passage and the rear opening is the anus leading into the rectum through which faeces (solid waste matter) leave the body.

All three of these openings have a tight ring of muscle around them to keep them closed. If it weren't there we'd all still need to wear nappies!

If the girl sits or lies with her legs apart and looks at herself with a mirror, she'll see that the front two of these openings are protected by two separate lips or ridges of flesh. These are called the labia. The outer ones are thicker and often hairy on the outside becoming mottled and darker on the inside. The inner pair of lips are thinner and sometimes knobbly in texture, varying in colour from light pink to dark, purplish brown. Sometimes the inner lips hang down below the outer lips and sometimes one side is longer than the other. Many girls get frightened by the colour or appearance of their labia and think there's something freakish or wrong with them. Girls

SEX – THE MECHANICS AND THE FUN

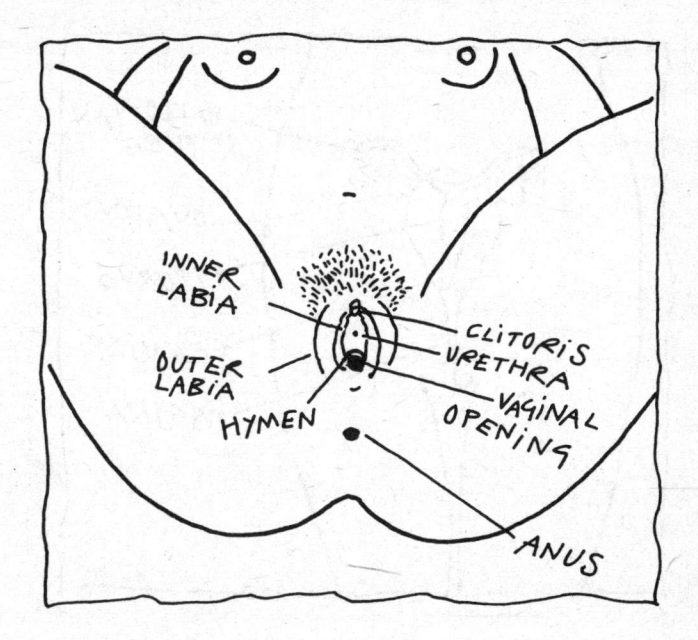

don't as a rule get much chance to see other women's genitalia (the outer sexual organs) but if they did, they would soon realise that every person is slightly different and be reassured that their own body was normal.

Still looking in the mirror she would be able to see that the two inner lips join together, at the front in a small fleshy bump. It's called the clitoris and is the key to female sexual arousal and satisfaction.

Girls – the inside

The vaginal entrance is partially protected by a thin layer of tissue called the hymen. If not already stretched by sport or exercise this may tear and even bleed when you have sex.

The vagina leads inside the body, pointing at a spot a couple of inches or so below the back of the waist. It's a tube with flabby, concertina-like walls which leads to the cervix. The cervix is a bulbous piece of muscle at the neck of the womb or the uterus. It

MAKING IT

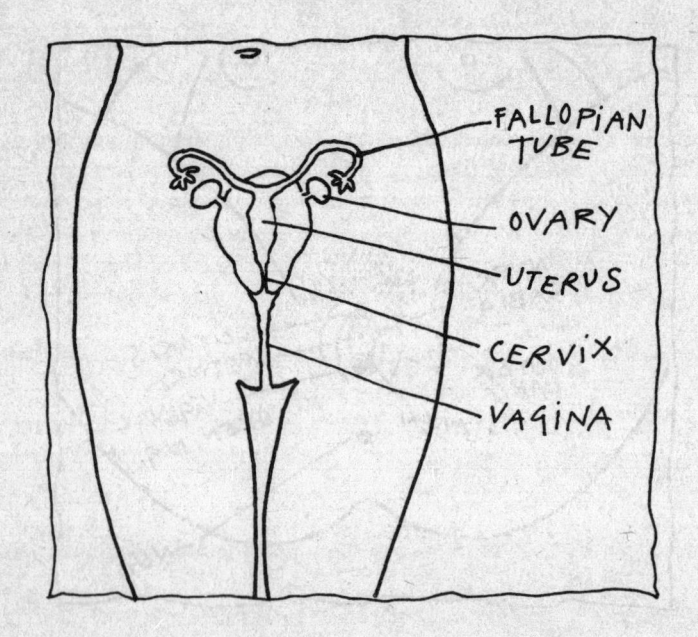

Diagram labeled: FALLOPIAN TUBE, OVARY, UTERUS, CERVIX, VAGINA

sticks down into the vagina and feels a bit like a rounded nose.

The further you go inside the vagina the fewer nerve endings there are. This means that a lot of sexual pleasure gained from having a penis inside the vagina is from the thrusting against the outer end of it and the stimulation of the clitoris.

Two tubes called fallopian tubes lead off the uterus and at the top of these are the ovaries.

Once a girl starts her periods the ovaries release an egg once a month (more or less taking it in turn) which passes down a fallopian tube into the uterus. This journey takes two or three days and if it isn't fertilised by a sperm during this time it dies and then passes out with other waste products from the uterus during the next period.

Boys – from the outside

The other big difference between boys and girls is that you can see a boy's sexual organs. They're hanging there; very hard to miss.

SEX – THE MECHANICS AND THE FUN

The tip of the penis is slightly pointed and the whole area around the end of the penis is thicker and bulbous. This is called the glans or the head of the penis. In most boys this area is protected by a fine piece of tissue called the foreskin. During intercourse this is pushed back exposing the end of the penis. Some boys have had their foreskins surgically removed leaving their penis less pointed looking. This is usually done because of ethnic or religious reasons but is sometimes necessary later on in adolescence when a boy's foreskin is too tight to allow him to have an erection without pain. The operation is called circumcision.

Many boys and men are very worried that their penises may not be big enough. They hear stories of 'superstuds' and sometimes watch 'adult' videos where every man is hugely endowed. In fact there is some variation in size of a normal unexcited penis but most erect ones are more or less the same size. Men seem to get particularly concerned with length whereas women, as I've described above, don't have all that much sensation at the top of their vaginas anyway. If you want to be a super lover then it's not the size of your penis that counts but how you use it!

Hanging behind the penis is a sort of bag of wrinkly skin containing the testicles or testes (or balls). The bag of skin is called the scrotum and it's usually hairy but you can still see the shape of the two testicles inside it quite clearly. This bit of the boy is exquisitely tender and often painful to touch. Most boys don't like their scrotum being touched at all, even during lovemaking.

A boy has only two openings in this part of his body. The first is at the tip of his penis and it's the opening of the urethra. This is the tube through which urine passes out from the bladder but it is also the sexual passage from which sperm emerge. Behind the scrotum, in the same place as in a girl, lies the anus or back passage.

Boys – the inside

The testicles produce and store sperm. When the boy becomes ready to ejaculate or come, the sperm pass up the tube (called the *vas deferens*) back towards the urethra. Near the base of the bladder they pass through the prostate gland where they mix with seminal

58 MAKING IT

[Illustration: UNCIRCUMCISED PENIS]

[Illustration: CIRCUMCISED PENIS]

fluid to form semen; a white, milky, slightly sticky liquid. You can't see the sperm swimming about in it because they're microscopic.

Girls know that they've reached puberty when they start to menstruate (have periods). The nearest equivalent for boys is their first 'wet dream'. This is when they wake up finding that they've had, during their sleep, an erection and ejaculated. They may remember having a sexy dream or they may remember nothing at all. Boys are capable of having erections from very early childhood but it's only when they get to the age of about 12 or 13 that they start to be able to ejaculate.

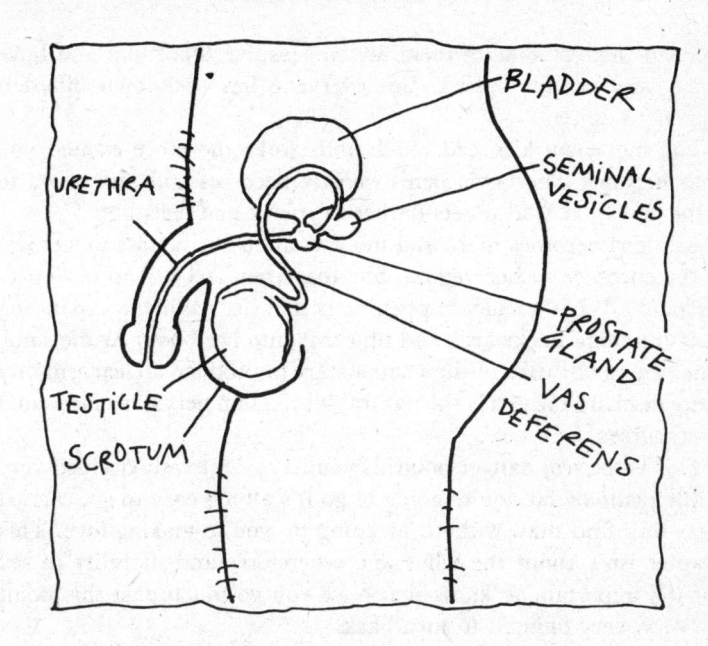

Feelings and sensations

So far, this has all been very factual, but what does it actually feel like?

Sexual arousal is a sliding scale. You don't only get sexually excited by touch and caress; sights, sounds, smells and memories can often do the job just as well.

Most young men start to get erections at the slightest excitement and they're aware of a stiffening and hardening in their penis, even if it doesn't eventually go all the way to a full erection. It often takes girls a bit longer to get to a similar stage.

Going a bit further up that rising scale of sexual arousal, you might find yourself touching or kissing your partner. The friction caused by kissing increases the blood flow to the lips and they seem to become warm and throbbing.

There are different areas in the body which are particularly sensitive to pleasurable sensations called erogenous zones. Apart from the area between your legs the obvious ones are your lips and your breasts. Like women, most men enjoy having their nipples touched though some of them are so sensitive there that you have to be very careful indeed. But everyone has their own different erogenous zones.

The more you kiss and touch and stroke the more excited you both become. The boy's penis quickly becomes stiff and starts to point upwards. It also gets darker in colour and feels hot.

As a girl becomes more and more aroused she'll start to feel wet at the entrance to her vagina. She may even feel it drip out on to her pants. What's really happening is that her vagina is expanding and stretching backwards and upwards into her body. At the same time, the inner walls of the vagina start to produce a clear, slightly slimy discharge which is the natural lubrication necessary for sexual intercourse.

This is the real danger point. If you haven't already decided very firmly just how far you're going to go it's all too easy to get carried away and find that, without meaning to, you're making love. This chapter isn't about the whys and wherefores and morality of sex but it's important to know that once you go much past this point it's very, very difficult to turn back.

Making love – foreplay

Let's assume that we are talking about a mature, adult relationship where a man and woman are going to go further than this and 'make love'. The touching and stroking that they are enjoying so much is called foreplay. Foreplay really starts with the first kiss but it goes on and develops until it is the touch of one naked body against another.

A man's penis is very obviously erect at this stage and he may want the woman to touch and stroke it. Doing this can sometimes cause a kind of stimulation overload and he may reach the point of orgasm before he means to. He is the best judge of the how much, where and when of every type of caress so it's up to him to let you know what feels good and bad. You don't have to talk about what you are doing in order to communicate this. He can just take your hand and move it as he wants you to move it or place it somewhere new, showing you what to do.

The opposite works too. A woman may discover at this point

that she wants to be stroked in the area around her clitoris and inside the opening of her vagina. Some men ignore the clitoris altogether (perhaps they don't know about it) and just try to put their fingers up inside the vagina as far as they will go. This can feel good but sometimes it hurts and in that case it is up to the woman to show her partner what she'd rather he did. Sometimes she may want him to rub hard and other times just gently tickle her. Only she can show him the rhythm and strength of touch needed.

Remember it's fine to experiment in love making but either partner should always be free to say, or to show by their actions, that they don't like something. **No one should ever be forced into doing something, or having something done to them, that they don't want**.

This involves a great deal of trust because it would be fairly easy for a man to carry on and try to force his penis into the woman. If you aren't able to discuss just how far you intend to go, then I don't think you've got any business to be having any sort of sexual relationship in the first place. Remember a sexual relationship involves responsibility; to yourself and to your partner.

You should also bear in mind that it is possible to get pregnant without full intercourse if the semen is passed into the vagina in some other way. So if you're going to arouse each other to orgasm without having intercourse, you should be careful that the man doesn't ejaculate anywhere near the woman's vagina or that none of the semen (and often a few drops appear before ejaculation) is accidentally transferred on the fingers to the vagina.

Making love – orgasm

Sexual intercourse is when a man puts his penis inside a woman's vagina and moves it up and down and in and out until he reaches orgasm and ejaculates. Interestingly enough, sexual intercourse doesn't necessarily involve orgasm for the woman. She may reach a climax at this point but, in biological terms, intercourse is just as successful (i.e. is just as likely to get her pregnant) whether she has one or not.

Many women are deeply disappointed that they don't automatically reach an orgasm at the same time as their partner. Some even feel they have failed in some way. But if you remember when I was describing the inside of the vagina, I said that there aren't all that many nerve endings deep inside. The girl gets most of her pleasurable sensation from the lower part of her vagina and around the clitoris so unless the penis is rubbing against the clitoris on its way in and out of the vagina, or at least exerting some tension on the skin surrounding it, she's very unlikely to reach an orgasm. In fact probably only about a quarter of women do reach an orgasm without being touched and caressed directly around the clitoris. For more on this, see the chapter on sexual problems.

But what is this sensation of orgasm or climax? It doesn't make it sound very romantic but it's actually like a sneeze and this is the same for both men and women. There's a point just before the sneeze (for me anyway) when it's really pleasurable to know that the sneeze is coming and there is nothing you or anyone can do to stop it. The tension increases and increases until it's released in a massive explosion.

It's just the same with orgasm. You are unable to see, hear or even think of anything else. Having an orgasm is a very private experience. Although many couples assume that they ought to be able to have one at exactly the same time and are disappointed when, like most people, they discover they can't, it is usually more satisfying for them to take it in turns. That way you can enjoy your own climax and enjoy seeing your partner have theirs.

What happens afterwards?

After the explosion of the orgasm there is a total relaxation of tension. Some men fall asleep for a few minutes or even longer. They can't help this; it's the way their body reacts to the strain that it has just gone through. Women sometimes don't appreciate this for they are more likely to want to cuddle up and even chat a bit. For both partners it's a time of a warm rosy glow when it's nice to rest, close together, while the body regains its strength.

Making love – the first time

I have just tried to describe what it's like to make love for two people who are in an established relationship and who are already at ease with their own and each other's bodies. But when it's your first time, things often don't go quite so smoothly.

Imagine a boy and girl, in love but both virgins. If they are sensible they may talk about sex, visit the family planning clinic together, maybe she goes on the Pill or they decide to use a condom but, at last, they find themselves in bed. However sure they are about what they are doing, they will both be nervous. They will both start to wonder if they really know how to 'do it' properly. The boy may be scared that he won't get an erection when he most needs it (and sometimes stage fright can make this happen) or, when he first touches the girl or she touches him, he may not be able to hold back and he ejaculates before they have even begun. This isn't the end of the world. The girl should take it as a compliment because it is his very desire for her that is causing his loss of control. The boy should be reassured that if he just rests for a few minutes, perhaps while hugging and kissing his partner, he will soon get hard again and, this time, the erection will last much longer.

The girl, meanwhile, may find that her nervousness is drying up her normal vaginal lubrication. When the boy touches her there she may feel irritated or sore, particularly if he rubs too hard. If this goes on it will be painful when he tries to insert his penis so one or other of them should apply some mild lubricant to the entrance to her vagina. KY jelly (from supermarkets or chemists) is fine but spit is just as good – and much cheaper. Don't use Vaseline or any petroleum-based product with a condom as it rots the rubber, causing them to split! Using a lubricant will ease the discomfort and encourage the walls of the vagina to start producing their own moisture again. She should also show the boy, by taking his hand or telling him, what feels good and what feels bad.

Eventually she may want to feel him inside her, and the boy will try to enter her. Sometimes this causes a panic because he can't find the hole! Poking away with his penis will only make the girl sore, so again one of them should put some KY or spit on the penis or around the outside of the girl's vagina and he, or she, should carefully take hold of the penis and guide it in. (If he is doing it, he might need to feel with his fingers, exactly where the opening is.)

If the girl's hymen has not already been stretched or broken by sport or exploratory fingers then she may feel a short sharp tearing pain. This will probably disappear almost immediately but, if it doesn't, the boy should be very gentle indeed. She may bleed a little and this might continue for an hour or two afterwards. Washing gently with warm water and wearing some tissue inside her pants will usually be all the 'first aid' that's needed.

Sexual intercourse, for the first time, may be awkward and painful. This is normal and is nothing to worry about. For further help see the chapter on sexual problems.

SEX – THE MECHANICS AND THE FUN

Different kinds of lovemaking

Mutual masturbation

Masturbation isn't just what you do to yourself in the privacy of your own bedroom. You can do it to someone else. Sometimes called 'heavy petting', it's a way of arousing your partner, and possibly giving them an orgasm, without actually having intercourse. Many couples who have decided that they don't want to go 'all the way' just yet can still give each other a great deal of pleasure. Remember too that it's important to discuss how far you intend to go. Petting sessions can turn into battle games of 'How far can I get him/her to go tonight?' unless both of you agree on some ground rules.

The big advantage of this kind of lovemaking is that it develops your sensuality. Once you have accepted that sex doesn't necessarily equal intercourse, you are free to discover many different ways of giving and receiving pleasure. People who believe that sex is no more than a quick kiss then a dive under the sheets miss out on all this and as a result their relationships are less likely to deepen and mature. In other words, you've got a better chance of holding on to your partner (male or female) if you put time and imagination into your sharing of pleasure than if you jump into bed and then think 'was that it?'

Finally, it's important to remember that this kind of lovemaking is much safer (in terms of pregnancy and sexually transmitted disease) than intercourse. In the age of AIDS, that could mean the difference between life and death.

Oral sex

Oral sex is when one partner uses their mouth to stimulate the other's genitals. This can be extremely pleasurable. Some women find that they are only able to get orgasms through oral sex though this is possibly because their partners are less gentle than they might be when it comes to intercourse or foreplay.

The technical terms are *fellatio* when a woman does it to a man and *cunnilingus* when a man does it to a woman. Fellatio is more commonly called a 'blow job' and some boys seem to ask girls to do this for them almost as a way of proving their dominance. When this happens it's no longer a loving action or even part of making love but simply a move in a power struggle.

Oral sex, or any other kind of sex, is okay provided both partners want to do it *and* enjoy it. No one should ever feel forced into doing something or blackmailed into 'proving their love' in this way. Many girls are repelled by the idea of oral sex and have enough trouble touching a penis with their hands, never mind their mouth. They're also very scared of gagging and choking on a penis and don't like the idea of taking the semen in their mouth when a boy ejaculates. In fact oral sex doesn't have to involve the woman taking the man's penis right into her mouth and throat. She can simply lick and kiss it and he can take care not to ejaculate in her mouth.

Some couples use oral sex as a way of having mutual pleasure and orgasm without risk of pregnancy. There's nothing wrong in this and you certainly can't get pregnant from it. However, sexually transmitted diseases including AIDS can be passed on by oral sex particularly if one partner has cuts or sores or ulcers in their mouth. (See the chapter on HIV and AIDS for more information.) And it goes without saying that unless both partners are scrupulous in their hygiene it can be a very unpleasant experience indeed!

Anal sex

Anal sex is when a man puts his penis inside his partner's (male or female) back passage or rectum. The anus is a very delicate area and the skin and tissue both outside and inside can be easily stretched and torn. Great care has to be taken and it's important to use some lubrication if trying it.

Because of the risk of germs entering the vagina and causing infection a man should never move his penis from one opening to the other.

Most important of all, though some people may think this is an outdated law, ANAL SEX BETWEEN MEN AND WOMEN IS ILLEGAL IN THE UK. This is true even between husband and wife. However, it is thought that many couples try it at some time or other, though most of them find that one experience relieves their curiosity and they don't bother again. Anal sex is legal between consenting male homosexuals, but only if they are both over the age of 21 (see page 22).

Saying no

In any sexual relationship both partners have to feel free to say no to anything they don't want to do. This may be because it offends them or because they just don't fancy it at that particular time. There are many old jokes about wives having 'headaches' every night but the fact is that in a long-term relationship, however much you love each other and are still turned on by each other's bodies and personalities, there are times when you just don't feel like making love. Thinking that you 'have to' because it's expected of you, can just make you feel worse and sometimes leads to a lot of friction and pressure between the two of you.

When you first fall in love and start a sexual relationship you may never be able to imagine a time when you won't want to be in bed with each other. However, one day it will happen that you're tired or worried or just generally preoccupied with something else and you want to say no. It's always better to say this straight out, and reassure your partner of your love, perhaps suggesting they ask you again tomorrow, than to make excuses or suddenly become very busy with your knitting or stamp album. And if your partner says 'no thanks' to you, don't go over the top and start accusing them of being unfaithful or falling out of love. Try to understand that they're just being honest in the same way that they hope you would be.

CHAPTER NINE

Contraception – the facts

Where do you get it?

You can buy some types of birth control, e.g. male and female condoms, spermicides and even the cap or diaphram if you know your size, from a chemist, but for everything else you have to see a doctor. That means either your GP, a family planning clinic or somewhere like a Brook Advisory Centre.

GP

You can go to any GP who provides contraceptive services and an up-to-date list of these is available from your local library. But if your doctor is your family GP, and you've known him a long time, it's very hard to tell him that you're thinking about having sex. You may be worried that he's going to tell your parents or at the very least give you an embarrassing lecture. As the law stands in England, Scotland and Wales, if you are over 16 your GP doesn't have the right to tell your parents without your consent; in fact, he or she must treat you as an adult. If you are younger it's slightly more complicated. A GP is only allowed to give you contraceptive treatment or advice if they consider that you are able to understand that advice and its implications. They are supposed to encourage you to speak to your parents and may suggest that you bring your mum in to the surgery so you can all discuss it. Whether or not they can actually go behind your back and tell your parents what you've asked is rather a grey area but most doctors say they wouldn't.

As one GP says:

'I'd rather see thousands of 15-year-olds for contraceptive advice than have one turn up pregnant. I personally don't inform parents but I do encourage teenagers to discuss it with them, for example I suggest if they were ill it might be important for someone to know they were on the Pill. If a parent asked me if their daughter was on the Pill I would say "ask her".

As far as the legal aspects of prescribing contraceptives to under-16s go, you either have to accept that a person is in effect an adult, in which case you give the Pill or whatever and you don't need to inform their parents, or they aren't adult enough to take the responsibility so you suggest that they talk to their parents or discuss it with their partner before going further. In neither case is it my place to contact their home and "inform" on them.'

You can see from this that some GPs may be more approachable than you imagine, but the whole business of talking about sex with someone who's been looking after you since you were a snotty-nosed 5-year-old can still be a bit much. So many girls opt to go to family planning clinics.

Family planning clinics

Find the address of your nearest clinic by looking in the *Yellow Pages* under Family Planning or (again) asking at your local library or ringing the head office of the Family Planning Association (071-636 7866). Most clinics have daytime and evening sessions and you should always ring first to make an appointment.

Clinics are for women who are taking responsibility for their own health. You'll find the atmosphere quite different to most doctors' surgeries because you talk to the nurses and the doctor on much more equal terms. No one tells you 'this is what you have to do'. All decisions are reached by mutual agreement between you and the staff.

What happens when I get there?

First, you see a nurse who'll ask you some questions about your medical history. The nurse will also weigh you, measure your height and check your blood pressure. You probably won't have an internal examination at your first visit and, even on later visits, you can always refuse. Lots of girls are worried about internals, feeling they'll either die of embarrassment or that it will be unbearably painful. Most of them are relieved when they discover it only takes about two minutes and is no more uncomfortable than inserting a tampon. Regular internal examinations and smear tests are the best way of protecting your sexual health particularly with regard to cervical cancer. (See the chapter on Sexual Health for more about this.)

After you've seen the nurse you'll be passed on to a doctor, nearly always a woman. She will discuss different methods of contraception with you and will give you some leaflets to look at. You'll find it's much less hurried than a normal GP consultation and you'll be encouraged to ask questions. Hopefully you will arrive at a joint decision about the best method of contraception for you. No pressure will be put on you to accept one particular method but equally she may say that, although you are dead keen, the Pill just wouldn't be right for you. In that case you have to listen to her because it's your health she's looking after.

CONTRACEPTION – THE FACTS

The good news is that all these services are free. Once you've decided on a method the clinic will give you a supply to last for about six months. You collect your next supply when you go back for a check up. REMEMBER though, you can go back at any time if you are not happy with your method or have any questions.

But what if I'm under 16?

The law is the same for family planning clinics as it is for GPs. They see many girls who are younger than 16 and they have to be sure that they understand the issues involved and are able to give 'informed consent' to the Pill or another form of contraception. But, as with a GP, the very fact that you've gone to ask for their help will say a lot about your level of maturity and, although they'll probably encourage you to consider the implications of having sex and discuss it with your mum or dad, they are very unlikely to go behind your back and tell your parents anything against your will.

What are the most common kinds of birth control?

Condom or sheath

This is the only reliable type of male birth control that we have. I'm going to talk about it first because I think it's the most important type of contraception around. As well as stopping you getting pregnant it also provides protection against sexually transmitted diseases including HIV. You can get more information on this in the chapter on HIV and AIDS, but my advice is that IF YOU'RE GOING TO HAVE SEX, WHATEVER OTHER CONTRACEPTION YOU USE, USE A CONDOM TOO! It may seem like overkill but in this case, where HIV and AIDS are concerned, 'kill' could be the operative word.

Many boys are put off using the condom because they say 'it's just not the same' but providing they use one of the extra sensitive types they'd have to have an almost super sensitive penis to feel any difference between making love with and without.

The condom is made of very thin rubber and it usually comes rolled up in a little foil sachet. The boy wears it over his erect (stiff)

72 **MAKING IT**

penis so that when he comes, the semen gets collected in the end of the condom and doesn't enter the girl's body.

For it to be reliable, it has to be used *very carefully* and the basic rules are as follows:

1. Pinch the little teat at the end of the condom before putting it on to the penis. This squeezes the air out of the teat leaving space for the semen when it spurts out.

2. Place it over the end of the penis and roll down the sides gently until the whole penis is covered.

3. Put it on as soon as the penis is erect, before there's any direct sexual contact with the vagina. This is because there are often a few drops of semen on the end of the penis long before ejaculation. It may not look a lot but it's more than enough to get a girl pregnant.
4. After his climax the boy should withdraw his penis from the vagina while it is still erect. As he does this he should hold on to the condom at the base of his penis, i.e. close to his body, so that it comes out with him. Be careful about close contact after this as there are still sperm lurking on the penis!
5. Take off the condom and tie a knot in the end, usually throwing it away wrapped in a tissue or something.
6. Use a new one each time you make love (sounds obvious but people do try to wash and dry them).

Condoms are designed to be used with an extra spermicide but in fact many types now available have a spermicidal lubricant already on them. If you're not sure about this have a look at the small print on the packet. IMPORTANT: Never use oil-based products, eg. Vaseline, body oils, bath oils etc, with a condom. They rot the rubber!

Advantages: Condoms are fairly cheap and they're easily available. You can buy them from chemists, supermarkets, many garages and machines in public loos. They're also available free from family planning clinics.

It's a way for a boy to show that he really cares about his girlfriend and for both partners to share the responsibility and the worry of contraception.

Disadvantages: Many people are put off by the fiddlyness and the embarrassment of it all. This often results in it not being used properly with consequent disasters.

One way to get over this is to make a feature of putting it on. It is undeniably fiddly but a couple can have a lot of fun at getting it on. Rather than turning away and furtively trying to get the packet open the boy can turn to the girl and say, 'Can you help.'

Also, because of the fiddlyness, it's wise to remember that practice makes perfect. You could either practise on yourself at home (now there's a hobby) or use something like a banana for a few trial runs. Think how pleased your mum will be when you start eating so much fruit!

It's also important to use a reliable type of condom – look for the British Standards Kite mark on the pack.

WITH CAREFUL USE (see guidelines on previous pages) condoms are about 98 per cent effective, i.e. about two in a hundred girls may get pregnant. WITH LESS CAREFUL USE the success rate can drop to about 85 per cent, meaning that up to 15 in a hundred girls who used condoms for a year could get pregnant.

The Pill

Lots of different brands are available but they fall into two main types; the combined Pill and the progestogen only Pill.

The combined Pill has been around the longest and, to put it simply, it works by fooling your body into thinking that it's already pregnant. This stops your ovaries from producing eggs once a month so there's nothing there to get fertilised if you do have sex.

The combined Pill and the progestogen only Pill alters the chemical balance inside your uterus so that an egg, even if it's lucky enough to get fertilised by a sperm, doesn't implant itself and grow into a baby.

Advantages: The big advantage is that it doesn't really seem to have anything to do with lovemaking. You take it every night or every morning when you clean your teeth and then you have nothing else to worry about. There are no awkward pauses when you say, 'Wait a minute while I just . . .' It also gives you a regular monthly cycle so you know exactly when you're going to have your period and it often makes periods much less painful and heavy.

Disadvantages: Some women have minor side effects much like you'd have in pregnancy e.g. nausea, headache, sore breasts, some weight gain.

Some things can interfere with the Pill working. If you have diarrhoea it may not be absorbed properly and of course if you vomit it won't have a chance to work. This means take care if you get drunk at parties! Some antibiotics and some tranquillisers can also affect the action of the Pill so if you are prescribed any medicines do check that they don't interact with the Pill.

CONTRACEPTION – THE FACTS

The Pill is one of the most reliable forms of contraception available. It's about 98 per cent effective IF TAKEN PROPERLY. That means that of 100 girls using it for a year and having regular sex, only about 2 would get pregnant. (Compared with 60–70 if no birth control was used.)

Injectible contraceptives
These act very like the progestogen only Pill. Progestogen is injected into your arm or leg, providing protection for two or three months. However, because of the large doses of hormone, it's only recommended for people who really can't cope with any other method. It's unlikely to be used for a young girl.

The intra-uterine device (IUD) or coil
The IUD is usually only recommended for women who have had children but there are a few types available which can be used with young girls if they and their doctors feel strongly it's the best type of contraception for them. Remember that the IUD does not give protection against HIV and other diseases.

The diaphragm or cap
Becoming more and more popular as women opt to come off the Pill. It's a 'barrier' method of contraception; forming a barrier or block between the cervix, which is the neck of the womb, and the invading sperm as they come swimming up the vagina. It must always be used with some kind of spermicide so that it not only blocks the entrance to the womb but kills off the sperm as they approach. It fits over the bulge of your cervix.

It is 85–97 per cent effective WITH CAREFUL USE (i.e. fitted properly and ALWAYS with a spermicide). At least 3–15 girls out of 100 would get pregnant, and some people can get an allergic reaction to the spermicide.

Female condom
The female condom (or Femidom) is the newest method of contraception available. It is made of thin polyurethane film rather like a large male condom but it covers the outer vaginal lips and entrance as well as going inside the vagina, protecting the vaginal walls and cervix.

Used properly it is probably quite reliable and it is the only female method to offer good protection against sexually transmitted diseases.

The sponge
Looks like a small doughnut which hasn't quite got a hole in the centre. It's made of polyurethane foam impregnated with spermicide. It's another barrier method and sits just in front of the cervix.

It is 75–91 per cent effective WITH CAREFUL USE i.e. at least 9–25 girls out of 100 would get pregnant. It can be bought from chemists but some people are allergic to the spermicide.

Natural methods
Based on the girl trying to predict when she will ovulate, i.e. when the egg is going to be released from her ovaries and can therefore get pregnant. This is usually approximately halfway between her periods but, in a younger girl or someone with irregular periods, it can vary quite a lot.

Early morning temperature can help predict ovulation as can the state of the natural mucus in the vagina.

This sort of birth control only has a chance of working if you have regular periods and you have to keep records for several months before you can start placing any reliability on it. Your partner has to understand that when you say 'not tonight' you don't just mean you've got a headache . . .

It's also important to realise that this method must be taught by a doctor or a family planning clinic, it's not something that you can rely on just sorting out for yourselves.

It's about 80–98 per cent effective WITH SKILLED AND CAREFUL USE i.e. about two to twenty would get pregnant.

Withdrawal or being careful
This is one of the least effective types of birth control around. It's also the most popular one amongst teenagers. It means that a boy tries to remove his penis from the girl's vagina before he gets to his climax.

If a boy ever says to you, 'Don't worry I'll look after you' or 'I'll be careful' you should ask him exactly what he means. I can't emphasise too strongly that this method is just too risky to be relied upon. It's a major disaster area.

There are three reasons for this. The first is that the boy nearly always releases a drop or two of semen, containing millions of sperm (literally), some time before he reaches his climax, so a girl can be well on her way to getting pregnant a long time before he even ejaculates.

Secondly, expecting a boy to withdraw his penis just at the moment of orgasm is like expecting a man dying of thirst in the desert to pour away a glass of water.

Finally, because expecting him to do that places such a strain on him, the whole business of using withdrawal as a method of contraception can start to come between a couple. They may find themselves picking all sorts of fights and niggling away at each other. Underneath it one or both is feeling resentful that they're not being satisfied during sex. AND IT ISN'T RELIABLE AT ALL!

Celibacy

A couple may decide that although they love each other and they're going to enjoy each other's bodies, they're not going to have intercourse. They can kiss and cuddle and stimulate each other to orgasm with loving caresses without the penis ever coming anywhere near the vagina.

If they trust one another this can be a good and pleasurable option but there is always the risk of being carried away and also of the transfer of some of the sperm into the vagina via someone's fingers.

Emergency contraception

Many people don't realise that this is available but, if you've inadvertently had unprotected sex or a sheath has burst or you've forgotten to take a Pill, using this service can save you weeks of worry. Emergency contraception is provided by any clinic or doctor who provides normal contraceptive services, but it has to be used within 72 hours of unprotected sex.

IT IS AN EMERGENCY, LAST RESORT MEASURE AND ISN'T SOMETHING THAT YOU SHOULD RELY UPON SO

THAT YOU DON'T WORRY ABOUT BIRTH CONTROL. In other words you can't keep on going and asking for emergency contraception month after month but, on the occasions when you need it, it's certainly very welcome.

What actually happens is that you either take a specially prescribed high dose of the combined pill or have an IUD inserted. With younger girls the pill is more likely to be prescribed and, because of the high levels of hormones in it, it may make you feel very nauseous, but you will probably be offered special anti-nausea tablets too.

Emergency contraception isn't always 100 per cent reliable so if you miss your next period or have any other signs of pregnancy you should still have a pregnancy test.

Myths about contraception

There are all sorts of Old Wives' Tales and myths about birth control. And it's amazing how many of us today still hang on to some of them. Here are some examples:

I can't get pregnant if I do it standing up.
YES YOU CAN

I can't get pregnant if I go to the loo straight afterwards.
YES YOU CAN

You can't get pregnant the first time you have sex.
YES YOU CAN

I can't get pregnant if I don't come (reach an orgasm).
YES YOU CAN

You can't get pregnant if you have a bath straight after sex.
YES YOU CAN

I can't get pregnant if he doesn't put his penis all the way in or he takes it out quickly.
YES YOU CAN

I won't get pregnant if we make love during my period.
IT'S UNLIKELY BUT NOT IMPOSSIBLE

Believing in any of these can seriously alter your life.

CHAPTER TEN

Being pregnant

How would you know you were pregnant?

A girl can only become pregnant if sperm from a boy's penis enters through her vagina and fertilises an egg inside her body. So if you have had unprotected sexual intercourse or heavy petting or fingering where some of the semen could have been transferred into your vagina, or even near the entrance of it, then you are at risk of being pregnant.

The first real sign is a late period. So it's a good idea to keep a record of the dates of your periods, just in case. However, pregnancy isn't the only reason for a late or missed period; sometimes worry and stress (for example, thinking you might be pregnant) can have the same effect.

The main thing to remember is that IF YOU KNOW YOU'VE TAKEN A RISK, THEN YOU COULD BE PREGNANT AND IT'S ALWAYS BEST TO FIND OUT FOR SURE.

So what should you do if you think you are pregnant?

Worrying about whether you really are or not is a waste of time and effort. If you're not pregnant it's just a pointless exercise in anxiety and if you are pregnant then you ought to be doing something practical about it; whether that's getting medical help for a healthy pregnancy or finding out about abortions. In other words, if you think you're pregnant, or there's even the slightest possibility that you might be pregnant, HAVE A PREGNANCY TEST. (And if your girlfriend thinks she's pregnant give her the same advice.)

Where can you get a pregnancy test?

GP
The obvious place to go is your GP but many girls are terrified of talking to their family doctors about this. They're scared that, even if they're not pregnant, it will get back to their family that they've been up to 'no good'. In fact, even if you're under 16 nearly every GP would always ask your permission before saying anything to your parents. They would encourage you to bring your mum into the surgery so the three of you could talk about it together.

So your GP can be a good person to go and talk to and, on the plus side, he or she can actually give you a pregnancy test free of charge.

Family planning clinic
If you are registered at a family planning clinic they can also give you a pregnancy test free. If you're not registered, they still may be able to do a test for you but you would probably have to pay. The easiest way to find out is to ring up and ask their policy. You can find the phone numbers of your local clinic either from the phone book, or a local library, or by ringing Family Planning Information Service in London (see the 'Contacts' section at the end of the book).

Pharmacists
Most pharmacists, or chemists, also offer pregnancy testing. You need to take in a sample of early morning urine (from the first time you go to the loo after you get up) in a clean jam jar or something similar. The results are usually available later the same day and pharmacists can be surprisingly discreet and helpful in giving you advice if you do find you're pregnant. Everything you say to them should be confidential.

'DIY' kits
You can also buy pregnancy testing kits at chemist's shops. Providing you follow the instructions very carefully, they give accurate results. The big snag is that they can be very expensive, often about £8 per kit. There are also a wide variety available and some of them

are now rather old-fashioned – and very complicated. Avoid the ones that say you have to use an early morning urine sample and go for the newer 'quick test' type. These can be done right from the first day your period is due, at any time of the day and they usually give results in a few minutes.

Even so, if you're going to use a DIY kit, do make sure that you can do the test in private. Choose somewhere where no one's going to walk in and interrupt you and you can have a few minutes on your own to get over the shock or the relief of the result. If your family doesn't have the type of bathroom that you can lock yourself into without everyone banging on the door then maybe you should consider taking the test kit round to a friend's house.

Private and charitable clinics
If you look in your local paper you'll probably see lots of ads offering pregnancy tests. Some of these are private clinics who charge a lot for their service and are hoping that if you are pregnant you'll have an abortion with them, paying even more! Always ring

first to check on fees before turning up with your bottle of urine or sending it in the post.

Other organisations like LIFE (see 'Contacts' section or look in the phone book) offer free pregnancy testing but don't necessarily make it clear in their advertisements that they are strongly opposed to abortion. If you think you might be pregnant and you know that you would consider abortion, you may find it less traumatic not to get involved with one of these organisations as they will put fairly strong pressure on you to go ahead and have the baby.

There are also charities like Brook Advisory, BPAS, and PAS (see 'Contacts' section) which run excellent counselling and medical services for women all over the country. They do charge for a pregnancy test but they also give unbiased counselling. If you want an abortion they'll help you arrange it, but they won't try to talk you into one if you want to keep the baby.

What happens if the test is negative?

Well, if the test shows that you're not pregnant you breathe a huge sigh of relief and promise yourself that you'll be more careful next time. With a bit of luck you will have had enough of a scare to get your act together and sort out a reliable method of contraception.

But, if you have a negative pregnancy test and your period still hasn't started seven days later, then you ought to have a repeat test. If both of these are negative but you miss a second period then you must see a doctor as soon as possible. Once you have missed two periods an internal examination will be able to tell a doctor whether or not you're pregnant. Pregnancy tests can sometimes be wrong and they're more likely to say you're not pregnant when you are than the other way round. So, if you're in any doubt at all, always see a doctor.

What if the test is positive?

It means you're pregnant and you have to start thinking fast.

Telling people

There's no way you can cope with an unplanned pregnancy on your own. You have to tell someone and get help soon. Get your mum on her own, take a deep breath and tell her what's wrong.

If you really can't talk to your mum then you ought to find another adult to confide in. Sometimes a friend's mother can act as go-between or maybe you have an aunt or cousin that you can talk to. Most doctors and family planning clinics will help you to talk to your parents or even act as go-betweens when tempers get high. A GP speaks:

'I know how scary it can be to talk to parents and I sometimes ask a girl to bring them into the surgery for some other reason and then I help her break the news to them here. They're still going to be angry but having me sitting on the other side of the desk can keep tempers down. The important thing is that we all understand the situation and get on with discussing where we go from here.'

It's also worth remembering that if you want to have an abortion you nearly always have to have the consent of one of your parents if you are under 16.

Telling your boyfriend isn't easy either. Maybe he already guessed and was waiting for the result of the test with bated breath and crossed fingers. But often the words 'I think I'm pregnant' fall like a bolt out of the blue. No one can predict how he'll behave. But try to remember that although it isn't him who's pregnant he will be frightened and very worried particularly if you're under 16 and he knows that he's been breaking the law.

Try to reassure him that this isn't the major problem at the moment. It's far more important to concentrate on what you're going to do and what the future of this baby is going to be.

Pretending it isn't happening

It can be very tempting to shove the whole idea of pregnancy to the back of your mind. Wearing loose clothes, eating less and generally keeping out of the way at home can even get you through most or all of your pregnancy without anyone realising what's going on, but the fact remains that eventually a baby is going to be born. Some girls even manage to ignore this and there are always tragic stories of new-born babies being dumped in rubbish tips or, more humanely, on police station steps or hospital entrances. Although being pregnant doesn't mean you are ill, you do need medical help and attention through the pregnancy and it's vital at the birth. Shutting your eyes to the problem or sticking your head in the sand doesn't make it go away. Pregnancy may not be what you wanted but it still has to be faced, later if not sooner.

'When I was working as a doctor in the local casualty department a 16-year-old girl with abdominal pain was brought in by her mum. When we examined her we found she was in labour, but she said she hadn't realised she was pregnant. She was in a curtained-off cubicle with her mum sitting in a chair outside the curtain. The baby was born and it started crying. Despite this she was still begging me not to tell her mum what had happened. It really is very difficult to know what to do . . .'

What if your girlfriend tells you she's pregnant?

However shocked you are and however frightened you may feel please try and give her your support. Assuming this pregnancy is unplanned, she's going to have some very difficult decisions to make and the very fact that she's pregnant makes her feel at her weakest and most vulnerable. Offering to accompany her to the doctor and talking through the options with her will all be appreciated.

Try to be honest about your own feelings and intentions. If you know that your relationship is already on the rocks and that a baby would definitely sink it then you should tell her. Hanging round with bunches of flowers and saying how sorry you are is being deliberately cruel and will only encourage her to think that the outlook is rosy.

If you can't see the three of you being a jolly happy family then you must say so now.

You must also realise that although you're the father of the baby you don't have any rights to influence her decision about abortion.

Making decisions

If you have an unplanned pregnancy you have several options open to you. You can try to have an abortion. You can have the baby and have it adopted. You can have the baby and keep it, either with your boyfriend or on your own.

The whole issue of abortion arouses very strong feelings in people. Even if it's something you've never thought much about yourself you may be surprised at how deeply you now feel one way or the other. Your parents and your boyfriend will try to influence you with their opinions but it's important that you really try to sort out for yourself what you want to do.

The big catch is that you have very little time. A pregnancy dates from the first day of your last proper period. So by the time you've missed two periods you are already at least 8 weeks pregnant. If you want to have an abortion it should ideally be done before you are 12, or at the very latest 16, weeks pregnant.

Abortion

What is abortion?
Abortion or termination means the ending of a pregnancy before the growing baby can live outside its mother's body. A miscarriage is a spontaneous abortion, something that occurs naturally and an induced abortion, or a termination, is one that is brought on deliberately.

When can you have an abortion?
A normal pregnancy lasts about 40 weeks, i.e. 40 weeks from the first day of your last period – not from the time you conceived. This works out at roughly nine months from the time you had sex to the estimated date of delivery (i.e. when you'll have the baby) and the length of the pregnancy is always calculated from the last period – a good reason to keep a record of your dates! In the UK (but not Ireland) abortions are technically legal up to 24 weeks of pregnancy, which is the point when a baby has a chance of living on its own. Because it's very often difficult to determine the actual number of weeks a woman has been pregnant abortions are, in practice, never

carried out after 22 weeks. But this is the extreme upper end of the range and it can be very difficult to arrange an abortion after 16 weeks of pregnancy. And sometimes even that is too late. A GP speaks:

'The snag is it's very difficult to get terminations of normal pregnancies under the NHS in our district after about 13 weeks. Locally we have a two-week waiting list before they can even be seen by a consultant, so 11 weeks pregnant is getting close to it.'

There are a few very rare occasions when abortions are carried out later, either because the baby is severely handicapped or the mother's life is at risk.

How would you go about getting an abortion?
To have an abortion in England, Scotland or Wales (they are illegal in Northern Ireland and Eire) two doctors must agree that your physical or mental state would be less damaged by an abortion than by going ahead with the pregnancy. In practice what this means is that you see one doctor who recommends you for an abortion and a second doctor, usually a gynaecologist, adds his consent to the form.

If you choose to go to see your GP, you may find him/her very sympathetic and able to help. They'll certainly have a good idea of how long your local hospital waiting lists are and they should be able to refer you for counselling in the meantime. They will also help you talk to your parents and discuss other options with you. But some GPs are opposed to abortion. In this case they are obliged to pass you on to another doctor or clinic who will be able to help you but, remember, every extra appointment takes time.

If you don't go to your GP in the first instance, you can go straight to any family planning clinic, Brook, BPAS, or PAS (see 'Contacts' section). They will offer you counselling and explain to you exactly what is entailed. Talking to one of these organisations doesn't commit you to having an abortion; the ultimate decision is always yours.

Because of health cuts and pressure, fewer and fewer abortions are now available under the NHS and those which are often have earlier limits set on them (see above). The alternative to the NHS is a private clinic. The charitable clinics run by BPAS and PAS operate to a high standard and although they do charge for their services, they always make allowances in cases of hardship. There are many other private nursing homes offering abortion but some of these charge extortionate rates and may not always offer adequate medical and counselling back-up services. I advise you to avoid the small ads for abortion services often found in the back of magazines and newspapers however convenient or appealing they may look.

How are abortions performed?

For pregnancies up to about 13 weeks, a suction method is used to remove the contents of the womb. This entails either a local anaesthetic with a few hours spent in the hospital or clinic or a general anaesthetic and an overnight stay. An alternative method is the 'D&C' which is when the cervix is stretched or dilated and the contents of the womb are gently scraped out.

After 13 weeks it's usually necessary to bring on a false labour so that the contents of the womb, including the unborn baby, are expelled through the vagina. This is done by injecting chemicals or putting chemical tablets inside the vagina and, as it causes very strong contractions, it can be painful. Painkillers are available and staff are usually very sympathetic, but it's still a traumatic experience.

In 1991 a new method of early abortion became available in England, Scotland and Wales. It's called Mifegyne, or the Abortion Pill, but it is only suitable UP TO THE NINTH WEEK OF PREGNANCY. It is a combination of pills and a pessary (a tablet that goes into the vagina) and it is not available from doctors or pharmacists, only licensed clinics and hospitals. If a woman doesn't stay within the clinic she has to be within easy reach as the pill causes bleeding like a very heavy period and, if there are complications, she has to be able to return for help.

How do you decide?

There is no easy way to make a decision about whether to have an abortion or not but you should be offered counselling by the doctor or clinic you approach. This will help you look at the options and examine your own feelings about pregnancy and abortion.

You may have strong religious views that mean it's out of the question, but in some ways that's easier because it determines the answer for you. It's much harder when you have to examine your own thoughts and feelings and decide what would be the best step. Some girls find that they just can't face the idea of an abortion and others, unfortunately, go through with it and then feel extremely guilty for many years. You'll also find that everyone else has their opinion too. The more people you discuss it with the harder it can get, but it's very important that you don't come to a decision just to please everyone else.

You will be under time pressure, but if you want more counselling then you must ask for it. It's always available and it's much better to be sure. Be aware that some so-called abortion counselling services are actually very anti-abortion, e.g. LIFE and Society for the Protection of the Unborn Child. While they will be sensitive and considerate to you, they will also try to persuade you to continue with the pregnancy and have the baby.

Only go ahead with an abortion if you're sure that is really what you want and what is best for you. Remember that you can change your mind right up to the last minute. Some girls get right into hospital before deciding to keep the baby after all.

What if I have an abortion and then regret it afterwards?

Many people do feel depressed after having an abortion and it's always best to talk about it. Family and friends attempt to push it to one side in an effort to cheer you up and help you get on with your life, but you may need time to grieve. Any of the clinics and charities offering abortion also offer post-abortion counselling and you're welcome to talk to them straightaway or even years afterwards if you feel bad. See the 'Contacts' section for further details.

Having the baby

If you decide to go ahead and have the baby I think it's important that you ask yourself what your motives are. Many girls, particularly those from unhappy homes, desperately want to have a baby just so they have 'someone they can love'. And, so they imagine, someone who will love them unreservedly back. If that's what you want then you should have a puppy!

Babies are tremendously demanding and they quickly become even more demanding and more difficult children. Is it possible that your reason for having a baby is selfish? Do you see it as the magic cure for your life, the one thing that's going to make you happy? If so, then I fear you'll be disappointed. Babies and children are wonderful but you have to have them and want them for their sake, not yours.

But if you are sure you want to go ahead and have the baby, nobody should be able to stop you. Some parents do try to apply a lot of pressure and force their daughters to have abortions but remember YOU HAVE THE RIGHT TO SAY 'NO'. Tell your doctor or the clinic how you feel, making it clear that you have thought about the options and definitely want to keep the baby.

You may be encouraged to give up your baby for adoption. You might hear the old argument 'but baby will have a much better home with Mr and Mrs X than he could ever have with you'. Maybe so. There are many couples who can't have their own children and who are desperate to adopt. Remember though, that even if you decide in favour of adoption during your pregnancy, you may feel totally different when your baby is born. In that case you can still change your mind.

Where do you live?

Many girls, even those whose parents have been furious and terrified at the beginning, live at home during their pregnancies.

Other girls go and live with their boyfriends or in their boyfriends' families' homes. At the time this may seem like an ideal solution but living together has its drawbacks as well as its advantages. Most couples go through a stage of hiccups and irritations before they settle down into a normal routine.

This is difficult enough to cope with if you've chosen to set up home together but if you find yourselves thrown together, particularly under his parents' roof, it's much worse. For some people it can be the right solution but if you have an alternative place to stay it might be worth waiting till you've had the baby before deciding whether or not you want to live together.

Some girls don't have supportive parents. They have no alternative but to leave home.

If this happens to you, there are two agencies that you should contact. The first is your local Social Services department. Either ring them up or walk into the local office and ask to see the duty social worker. Some girls cherish illusions that Social Services will set them up in a nice little flat. It doesn't often work like that. But they will try to find you temporary accommodation, possibly with a foster family if you're 17 or under, or in a bedsit or hostel. They should also be able to give you information on any voluntary and charitable agencies in your area.

The second agency which does a tremendous amount of work for young pregnant girls is LIFE. They are highly opposed to abortion but they give practical and emotional support to anyone who wants to keep their baby. You can find the address of their head office in the 'Contacts' section at the end of this book but they have local branches all over the country. Often these are listed in the phone book or advertised in the personal columns of local papers.

LIFE can offer you a befriending and counselling service even if you live at home through your pregnancy but they also have families who will take in pregnant girls as well as their own mother-and-baby hostels.

Should we get married?

Despite what your parents, and other people may say, you shouldn't feel that you *have* to get married just for the baby's sake. If either of you enters marriage seeing it as a trap, you haven't much hope of making it last. Teenage marriages have one of the highest divorce rates of any age group. Some boys are suspicious that their girlfriends became pregnant 'accidentally on purpose' in order to push the issue of marriage. In some cases their suspicions are probably justified. In this situation wouldn't it be better to wait until after the baby is born, and the pressure dies down, before deciding whether or not to make life-long vows?

'When I found I was pregnant I really wanted to get married. I wanted to walk down the aisle in white – bump and all! But he wasn't keen. Looking back I can see he was terrified. He never exactly said no but he just kept avoiding the issue and putting it off. It wasn't until after she was born that I realised he'd hardly taken any interest in the pregnancy and that there was no way he was going to turn into a regular father. It seemed like we had nothing in common anymore.'

As the law stands at present, you have to be at least 16 in order to marry and, in England, Wales and Northern Ireland, if you are under 18, you must also have your parents' permission.

CHAPTER ELEVEN

Sexual health

Sexual hygiene

Girls

It's important to know that most healthy vaginas have a discharge. This discharge is normal and it has its own peculiar but inoffensive smell. It varies according to the time of month, getting stringy and jelly-like approximately halfway between your periods (this is when you ovulate) and thicker and whiter before your period starts. You should only worry if it becomes yellow or green, itchy or very strong smelling. This indicates some sort of infection, e.g. thrush and you should always consult a doctor.

To keep your genital area clean, wash morning and evening with warm water and a mild soap. Avoid strong soap, body lotions or talcum powders as perfume or colouring can lead to problems like thrush. It used to be fashionable to use vaginal deodorants or douches (squirting soapy or perfumed water inside the vagina) but this is now known to be dangerous and is unnecessary anyway.

When going to the lavatory it's a good idea to wipe off any drops of urine with a tissue as this can quickly cause an unpleasant, stale odour and after emptying your bowels you should always wipe your bottom from front to back. This prevents any germs being pushed forward into your vagina where they could cause an infection.

During your period it's important to change your towel or tampon regularly, i.e. at least four times a day. It is as important to bath or wash regularly during your period as it is at any other time.

Boys

A normal uncircumcised penis produces a white, waxy substance underneath the foreskin. This is called 'smegma'. If it is left to collect and 'ripen' it smells a bit like old cheese and can cause irritation and infection. To prevent this boys should push their foreskin back carefully and wash their penis thoroughly in warm water and a mild soap every day. Boys who've been circumcised, i.e. don't have a foreskin, may still produce some traces of smegma so they should also take care to keep their penis clean.

Hygiene before and after sex

Some people, girls in particular, get very hung up about their natural body odours and are scared that their partners will be turned off by these very normal smells. This isn't true. A healthy vagina does give off its own particular smell, especially when it's sexually aroused, but this isn't dirty or bad in any way. It actually acts as a turn on to men. So there's no need to spend an hour in the bath scrubbing yourself from head to toe before going to bed with someone.

Common health problems

Worries about breasts

Many girls worry that their breasts are too small or too big or that one side is larger than the other. Most people come to terms with accepting what they have but a few, often because of thoughtless comments at home or name-calling at school, get badly hung up about it. The girl with large floppy breasts will often loathe sport at school because of all the comments she attracts from boys and she may lack self-confidence in relationships because she can't believe that a boy sees any more to her than '38C'.

A girl with tiny breasts may worry that she is somehow unfeminine or not developing properly. The fact is that everyone's body is individual and just as people have different sized hands and feet so they have different sized and shaped breasts. And just as it's common for one foot to be a bit larger than the other or one ear to stick out more, so a right breast may be different to a left breast.

If you have these sorts of worries try to believe that you are far more aware of the problem than anyone else. Ask your mother, your friends or even your doctor for reassurance.

Penis problems

NB. This section deals with physical problems of the penis. See the next chapter on Sexual Problems for things like difficulties with erection and coming too quickly.

Infections under the foreskin: If you aren't careful about washing underneath your foreskin you can develop infections. This causes the end of the penis to become red, swollen and painful. If this happens to you, see your doctor straightaway and he'll give you some ointment and/or pills to cure it.

Lumps in the scrotum: Most boys (and men) find that one of their testicles hangs slightly lower than the other. Sometimes one is also a little larger than the other. This is all normal but if the height or size of one starts to alter then they should always have it checked. Sometimes small lumps or large swellings can appear. Again these should always be checked by a doctor because although they're quite likely to be some minor infection or inflammation there's always the chance that they could be more serious. Early treatment is always the safest and the best.

Oddly shaped or crooked penis: Many boys worry about the size of their penis. This is nearly always unnecessary as you can see in the section on boys' bodies in the chapter 'Sex – the mechanics and the fun'. Other boys get very uptight because their penis is crooked or oddly shaped. In fact, an erect penis often bends either to the left or the right or points slightly up or down. This shouldn't make any difference to your ability to make love.

Bleeding from the penis: This could be caused by something quite simple like a burst blood vessel but as there's a slight chance that it could be a sign of some more serious internal disease, you should see a doctor.

Infections of the vagina and penis

Most of these infections affect both boys and girls although often the symptoms are more likely to be noticed in one sex than the other. Most can be passed on by having sex although some of them, particularly cystitis and thrush, can also occur in someone who's never had any sexual contact at all.

Cystitis: Cystitis is infection and inflammation of the bladder and urethra. It can be spread by sex but it often occurs seemingly out of the blue. A passionate bout of lovemaking can bring it on because the urethra becomes bruised, leaving it more prone to infection. Bad genital hygiene and wiping your bottom from back to front can also cause germs to be passed from the anus into the urethra.

Women suffer from cystitis more than men. The symptoms include a feeling that you need to pee every few minutes, pain when you do go to the loo and a stinging sensation afterwards. Some people get a slight fever or backache with it as well.

Cystitis can be cleared up with antibiotics or other medicines from your doctor and you should always go to get help if you think you have an attack. Leaving cystitis will only make it worse and also give the chance for the infection to pass up into your kidneys.

Urethritis (or NSU Non-specific urethritis): This is more common in men though women may suffer from it without knowing because they have no symptoms. It is an infection of the urethra and causes pain and burning in a man's penis when he tries to pass urine. The symptoms are similar to those of cystitis. It can be transmitted through sex so if the man is suffering his partner should also be treated as she may re-infect him once he has been cured.

Most types of urethritis ('non-specific' just means that the cause

SEXUAL HEALTH

isn't known) can be treated with antibiotics. See a doctor as soon as possible.

Thrush: Thrush is a common problem affecting the majority of women at some time. Inside the vagina grows a natural yeast-like substance which helps the vagina keep itself clean and fresh. However, if the chemical conditions are upset or unbalanced, e.g., by strong bath oils or some antibiotics, this yeast can get out of control and cause a heavy white, cheesy discharge. It can also cause excruciating itching where the sufferer wants to tear off her clothes and scratch herself raw. As the inflammation spreads it also causes pain on passing urine.

Thrush can be difficult to cure and it's best to seek help as soon as possible. Your doctor will probably prescribe ointment or pessaries (waxy pellets to put into the vagina) and it's important that you always finish the course of these even if the symptoms disappear first. Some women find relief from thrush by inserting dollops of natural live yoghurt into their vagina on the end of a tampon. They do this several times a day for three or four days. The bacteria in the yoghurt (and it must be 'live' yoghurt not pasteurised strawberry flavour) help to keep the yeast organisms under control.

Genital herpes: Genital herpes is caused by a virus closely related to the one that gives you cold sores. It's nearly always spread by sexual intercourse or at least close sexual contact and recently there's been a lot of publicity and scare stories about it.

It's an unpleasant and painful disease and at the moment there's no positive cure for it. About half of all sufferers never have more than one attack but, if you are one of the unlucky half, with the right drugs and self-help routines, you can control outbreaks so that they are less painful and more short-lived.

The first symptoms of an attack are tiny blisters on or inside the genitals. You may not notice them but the blisters burst leaving ulcers which cause a lot of pain and take two or three weeks to heal. During this time it would probably hurt to pass urine and sex would be painful. You may also get symptoms of feverishness and swollen glands in the groin. If you think you have herpes you should see a doctor.

You should never have sex during or immediately after an attack of herpes. Remember this includes not only intercourse but close sexual contact of any kind. Some people seem to catch a type of genital herpes from cold sores on the mouth. It isn't quite as severe as the virus described above but it's still unpleasant. If you suffer from cold sores keep your mouth to yourself until they've cleared up.

Warts: Genital or venereal warts appear around the genital area in both men and women. They are ordinary warts and can be passed on by sexual contact or can occur on their own. They start off tiny and they quickly grow to a sort of cauliflower shaped lump about the size of the end of your little finger. They usually aren't painful but they itch and, as they're spread by touch, scratching isn't a very good idea.

Warts can be treated by applying a special lotion to shrink or burn them off. This has to be done with great care under medical supervision, i.e. you must see a doctor.

Pubic lice or crabs: Pubic lice are cousins of the head louse. They are spread by sexual contact or from infected towels and bedding. Once you've got them, they cling on like crazy. It's very hard to remove them with ordinary washing and contrary to popular opinion, they actually prefer clean skin.

If you are infected you will probably be able to see tiny (about 2mm long) brown or white insects in your pubic hair.

You can buy lotions and shampoos to get rid of lice over the pharmacist's counter and if you use these it's very important that you follow the instructions carefully. But, if this doesn't work or you don't want to talk to a pharmacist about it you would be better off seeing your doctor.

Gonorrhoea (the clap or a dose): Together with Syphilis is the correct name for what used to be called venereal disease (VD). It can only be caught by intimate body contact, not from loo seats, towels, etc.

Men who are infected with gonorrhoea usually feel pain when they pass urine. They may also have a yellow discharge. The symptoms start between two and ten days after infection. Eventually symptoms may go away and, particularly if he's been trying to put off the idea of seeing a doctor, the man may breathe a sigh of relief and put the problem out of his mind. Unfortunately, that isn't the

SEXUAL HEALTH

end of the matter. Gonorrhoea has spread deeper inside and, sooner or later, will cause inflammation in the internal sex organs. It could even lead to infertility.

A woman often doesn't have any symptoms at all. Any slight discharge may not be noticed amidst her normal vaginal discharge. The only reason a woman may know she has gonorrhoea is either because a sexual partner tells her he is infected, or when several weeks or even months later, she has severe pain and inflammation in her lower abdomen. This too can lead to infertility.

The best way of avoiding gonorrhoea is restricting the number of sexual partners you have and practising safe sex. More about this later in the section on AIDS.

Syphilis (or the Pox): Is the other well known variety of 'VD'. Rarer than gonorrhoea but still around. What's more, it can kill you if it's left untreated.

Like gonorrhoea it's only caught by intimate sexual contact and its symptoms appear in set stages.

The first stage is a small painless sore that looks like a mouth ulcer and appears somewhere on the genital organs. It may be on the outside or the inside. As it doesn't hurt it can often go unnoticed and, after a week or so, it goes away.

As the initial sore disappears the syphilis starts to invade the bloodstream causing symptoms all around the body. These include aches and pains, fever, rashes etc. They're often confused with flu or other viral infections. Eventually, these symptoms fade away.

The disease then lies dormant before eventually lurking there multiplying and attacking different organs. Often the first time someone knows they have syphilis is when they are admitted to hospital with some serious problem with their heart, liver, kidneys or even brain.

Getting help

Your GP will help you with any of these problems. Remember that whatever you say to him is kept in confidence and won't be told to anyone else. Even if you're under 16 he shouldn't say anything to your parents without your consent.

There are also special clinics in major hospitals. These are often called GUM (Genito-Urinary Medicine) or STD (Sexually Transmitted Disease) Clinics. Different health authorities call them different things but you can find the address and telephone number of your nearest one by ringing up your local hospital and asking for the number of the Special Clinic or by looking in the telephone book under Sexually Transmitted Diseases.

Most of these clinics run an appointments system although you nearly always manage to get an appointment within a couple of days. When you get there you're given a number to save the embarrassment of having your name called out in the waiting room. You'll be seen by a nurse and a doctor and you should be prepared to describe your symptoms and say whether you've been having sex recently or not. You'll be examined and will probably have to give a urine sample and a blood sample. If you do have a serious infection like gonorrhoea, syphilis or HIV you'll be asked to give the names of your sexual partners so that they can be contacted and invited in for testing.

Some results will be available straightaway while others can take up to a week. Testing and all treatment is free. All services of these clinics are completely confidential – whatever your age, and you can even ask for your GP not to be informed.

CHAPTER TWELVE

HIV and AIDS

We've all heard a lot about HIV and AIDS over the last few years; so much so that many of us don't really bother to listen any more. Yes, AIDS is scary, but it's not going to affect us. OR WILL IT?

What is AIDS?

AIDS stands for Acquired Immune Deficiency Syndrome. This means it's a group of symptoms or diseases (the syndrome bit) caused by a breakdown in the body's protective immune system (the immune deficiency part) which can be transmitted from person to person (i.e. acquired). AIDS is an illness which destroys the part of the body that fights off other illnesses. So people don't actually die of AIDS; they die of different mixtures of diseases and conditions that AIDS allows them to develop.

What about HIV?

HIV stands for Human Immuno-deficiency Virus. A virus is a small type of germ, similar to the kind that might give you flu, but in this case it attacks the human immune system. It's the virus that gets transmitted from person to person, so people catch HIV, not AIDS.

Does having HIV mean you're going to get AIDS?

No, not necessarily – or at least we don't think so. But it seems likely that just about everyone who does develop AIDS will eventually die of it. One of the problems is that we don't really know how many people have HIV. The only way to be sure is to test their blood for antibodies to the virus. If these are present, then the person is HIV positive (HIV+). Research projects suggest that as many as ten million people may be HIV+ worldwide. Each of them is capable of transmitting the virus on to others and is also at risk of developing AIDS. It is possible that some of them will never get AIDS but, at present, experts think the majority will do so.

How is HIV transmitted?

The virus is transmitted either via the blood or a sexual body fluid, i.e. semen or vaginal or cervical secretions. That means the main ways of catching HIV are through unprotected sex or through sharing needles and works with an infected drug user.

In the past, some people were infected by blood transfusions but now all blood in the UK is screened before being used, although this may not be true in other countries. HIV can also be passed on from an infected mother to an unborn child, although many HIV positive mothers have had healthy babies. There is also a risk of infection through breast milk.

But surely only gays get it?

When HIV and AIDS were first discovered most cases in the Western world (i.e. USA and UK) were amongst male homosexuals. Some people even called it a 'gay plague'. But the rate of spread has now slowed down in the gay population, mainly because people are taking more care and precautions.

Worldwide, more women than men suffer from HIV and AIDS and in Third World countries it has spread rapidly through straight but unprotected sex. It seems that women are more vulnerable than men and the virus passes to them more readily.

Why is sex so dangerous?

If someone is HIV+, their sexual body fluids (semen and vaginal fluid) contain a fairly high concentration of HIV. During intercourse these can be transmitted directly to the partner's body, putting them at risk. They wouldn't necessarily catch HIV the first time they had sex but they could, and the more they do it the greater the danger.

The risk increases if there is any contact between the sexual fluids and the bloodstream of the partner. This is why HIV spread very rapidly amongst the gay populations where anal sex often caused breaking of blood vessels in the anus (back passage), resulting in the mixing of semen and blood. But cuts, grazes, vaginal infections like thrush or open sores like herpes can also be a danger. The only way to protect yourself is either to avoid intercourse or to make sure you always use a condom.

What about oral sex?

Oral sex (blow jobs, going down, etc) is safer in terms of HIV than intercourse because gastric juices are pretty powerful in killing off any swallowed virus before it can do any damage. There may be some virus present in saliva (see below) but there's no evidence that it is in a concentrated or active enough form to be dangerous. However, there could be a very real risk if you have cuts or sores or ulcers in or around your mouth. If the virus is present in your partner's vaginal fluids or semen it could then be passed directly into your bloodstream via the openings in your skin.

But what about all the other ways of catching HIV?

There aren't really any other ways. HIV is a very fragile virus and it dies off soon after it's been exposed to air. It is present in other parts of the body, but not in any great concentration. Although scientists have been able to detect it in tear fluid or saliva, there is no evidence that these have ever been a route of infection. So it's perfectly safe to share cups and glasses, etc., with someone who's HIV+. You can't get it from shaking their hands or hugging them either. Nor from mosquito bites, loo seats, door handles, towels, bus seats or any of the other ways that crop up in silly scare stories.

So how can you protect yourself?

Avoid injecting drugs and stick to safer sex. That means making sure you never have intercourse (penis in the vagina or penis in the anus) unless you are protected by a male or female condom (see the section on contraception on page 71 for more information). It's also a good idea to develop a wider sexual repertoire so that you don't fall into the very boring habit of assuming that intercourse is the only 'proper' type of sex.

There are many other ways of touching and sharing pleasure that don't involve penetration. If you don't believe me, think back to the early days of petting or go and have a look at some sexy manuals in the book shop. Two people in love can really get off on mutual erotic massage and there's nothing to stop each of them reaching a climax with the help of their own or their partner's fingers. It's fun, it's safe and it doesn't get the girl pregnant either!

If you are going to use a condom, make sure you use it properly. Remember the penis can release some pre-cum, a drop of semen, long before ejaculation. Put the condom on as soon as the penis is erect and check that it has added spermicide, preferably Nonoxynol 9 (look on the packet), because this seems to have an effect in killing off the virus. However, if you or your partner develops an allergy or a reaction to the spermicide, then switch to another type of sheath or avoid sex for a while. Remember, if an allergy causes itching or scratching of the genital area, it can leave you raw and more open to infection.

That's ok for one-night stands, but what about someone you know and love?

It's great to be in love and able to trust someone but can you trust their previous partners and all *their* previous partners? Say you're a bloke and about to sleep with a girl and she's only ever slept with one man before. But he's had four girlfriends and each of those has slept with three men. That means already you are having a kind of sexual contact with at least 18 people. If you work it out for several more stages the risk can be mindblowing.

YOU CAN'T TELL IF SOMEONE IS HIV POSITIVE. They

look just like you, me or anyone else. It's not enough being in love and talking about your sexual pasts (even if everyone was always totally honest about this) because we can't speak for our partners' partners' partners and you have to accept that you are just one point on a very complex web of connections. So, yes, do take care on one-night stands but take just as much care with the person you love. After all, surely they deserve it?

What about HIV tests?

Anyone who is worried about HIV can arrange to have a free blood test, although they're always advised to have counselling beforehand. There are various reasons for this. Firstly, a blood test looks for the presence of antibodies to HIV in the bloodstream, showing whether or not the body has been infected with the virus. But it takes a while for antibodies to develop, often up to three months after infection, so having a blood test with a negative result (i.e. no antibodies) means that you weren't infected up to about three months ago. Of course, if you've put yourself at risk since then, another blood test would be advisable in the future. As you can see, having endless blood tests isn't the answer; DOING SOMETHING ABOUT YOUR BEHAVIOUR MIGHT JUST SAVE YOUR LIFE.

Having the test may have implications later on in your life when you want to get a mortgage or life insurance. At present some companies penalise you if you admit to having had an HIV test; regardless of the results. You can get more information about this and any other questions about AIDS and HIV from the National AIDS Helpline (see the 'Contacts' section), or from the nearest special or GUM clinic (see pages 99–100).

How do you cope with being HIV positive?

The first thing to remember is that having HIV doesn't necessarily mean to say that you're going to get AIDS. So you're unlikely to feel ill straightaway. You will feel scared and isolated. Being HIV positive cuts you off from the rest of the world. The shock of the discovery and the fear of what may happen can turn people in on themselves, making the situation worse. Unfortunately there's a lot of prejudice around about HIV and AIDS and announcing the fact to the world in general is likely to cause, at the very least, unpleasant and unhelpful comments. There have been cases of children being withdrawn from schools because of rumours that one of their co-pupils was infected with the virus. This is obviously pointless and ridiculous because if you've read this far you'll know by now that HIV can't be caught by working, playing or eating together.

So if you or someone you know is HIV positive it's important that they find someone that they can talk with to help them break out of their isolation. There are many organisations offering excellent counselling for this and you can find details in the 'Contacts' section.

If you discover that a friend or family member is HIV positive, try to give them as much support as you can. A big hug can make them feel a whole lot better! One of the ways of combating the onset of AIDS is to keep as healthy as possible and someone infected with HIV should try to eat a full sensible diet, take regular exercise

HIV AND AIDS

and a generous amount of rest. Avoiding too many stresses and strains also helps the body fight off illness. But sometimes it's very hard for someone to make the effort to take that much care of themselves. Saying how much you love and value them will encourage them, bringing you closer together.

You may be scared that you have been infected as well. In that case, you should talk to an AIDS counsellor as soon as possible. They can tell you more about the AIDS test and arrange for you to have one, if that's what you decide to do.

CHAPTER THIRTEEN

Sexual problems

This chapter is about some of the sexual problems that can occur in even the best relationship. It assumes that anyone needing this kind of help will be old enough, and mature enough (not necessarily the same thing) to appreciate and take full responsibility for their sexuality. That means protecting themselves and their partner from unwanted pregnancy, disease and emotional blackmail. These problems may not apply to you now but you may find it useful to know about these problems in case you meet them later on.

Some things, like premature ejaculation i.e. coming too quickly, happen to most men at least once in their lives, while others are less common. This chapter gives advice on what you can do to remedy the problem yourself and where to turn for expert support when self-help doesn't seem to be the answer.

The ups and downs of sexual arousal

Before talking about problems that can affect your sex life, it's important to understand a little bit about how sexual arousal works. Basically, we can be aroused in two ways. There's the obvious direct physical stimulation that goes on during good, harmonious lovemaking. But there's also an important component of mental stimulation – thinking sexy thoughts if you like. If someone isn't in the mood for sex, then they really aren't in the mood. It's very hard indeed to get turned on if you're preoccupied with something else.

Just as either of these types of stimulation can cause you to become sexually aroused, so a blockage of stimulation or actual negative stimulations would prevent arousal altogether. It's a bit like a game of snakes and ladders. If you imagine the sexual arousal as a ladder with the target of orgasm at the top, you need to have everything right, both physically and mentally, before you can start climbing the rungs. If something goes wrong then you miss a rung and end up sliding down the slippery snake. In real terms, this means a woman may not feel turned on, and her vagina may not enlarge and produce the lubrication necessary for sex, making intercourse painful. If a man starts to slide down the snake the effects are even more obvious; his erection wilts.

So what sorts of thing cause these blockages or negative stimulations? Well, on the physical side, anything that hurts can be an immediate turn-off. Different people have different pain thresholds and some people like being touched in one place while others hate it, but there are obvious things that can cause pain and which are best avoided during lovemaking. Most men don't like having their testicles squeezed (don't try it, just take my word for it) and it can be very uncomfortable for a woman if a man tries to push his fingers or his penis inside her vagina before she has become aroused enough to be moist and ready for him. If a man tries to finger a woman's vagina with torn or ragged nails he can cut or scratch her without realising it.

There is an enormous variety of things that can interfere with mental stimulation. Any of the negative emotions, e.g. anger, resentment, worry and fear can stop you feeling sexy. Preoccupation, whether it's worrying about the coming exams or just wondering what you should wear to the party on Saturday, can also do the trick. The anxiety that comes from being under pressure, for example when your partner is expecting you to perform in a particular way or to reach a spectacular orgasm, is also a tremendous downer. So is simple tiredness.

When you consider the effect that all these emotions can have on sex it's hardly surprising that when a couple consult a sexual or marital therapist with a sexual problem the first thing the therapist wants to know about is usually their relationship. Tension and friction in an established relationship nearly always results in sexual symptoms. There's no point in putting a sticking plaster on the sex problem if the relationship one still exists.

Common female problems

Pain or discomfort during intercourse

If this happens at the beginning of a sexual relationship, it's most likely caused by unpractised lovemaking. It may be that your partner is taking things too quickly and trying to force his way into your vagina before you are fully aroused and lubricated. Ask him to slow down and encourage him to spend more time on kissing and hugging and stroking, i.e. foreplay, before entering you. Using some extra lubrication like KY jelly or spit will make things much easier. You don't need to worry that using something like this will turn lovemaking into a clinical procedure; you can rub it on his penis first. I can assure you that he won't mind!

If it's your first sexual experience then the pain may be caused by the stretching and tearing of your hymen, i.e. the loss of your virginity. This can be sore and you'll probably bleed a bit. Again, gentle, gradual lovemaking will result in gentle, gradual stretching rather than sudden, rough tearing. If your partner cares for you he'll be guided by you and if you appear to be in pain he should stop and withdraw. But remember, it's up to you to tell him if it hurts. He's not a mind reader!

Some women experience pain deep inside them during sex. This can be the result of the penis bumping against the cervix or even prodding their ovaries through the vaginal wall. It's usually not dangerous but the sensation can be off-putting. You may find that changing your lovemaking position will help things. For example, you could lie side-by-side or kneel on top of him for a change.

If none of these helps and the pain persists, or if you regularly bleed after intercourse, then you should always see your doctor or family planning clinic. It could be a warning sign of some kind of growth (don't panic, the majority of them are harmless and not cancer) on your cervix or other pelvic organs.

Penis can't fit into the vagina

Some women find that however much in love and aroused they are, they just can't have sex. The penis seems to hit a solid wall of flesh and the woman feels nothing but pain. Most couples with this problem give up attempting intercourse and stick to mutual masturbation instead – but it can be helped.

In fact, a normal vagina can accommodate any size or shape of normal penis. If you remember the section on girls' bodies in 'Sex – the mechanics and the fun' you will know that the vagina is a concertina-like tube which enlarges and balloons out during sexual arousal. Around the outer third of it is a thick, muscular band which can sometimes go into spasm and close the entrance to the vagina. It's this effect that causes the above problem. The medical name for it is vaginismus.

Sometimes, you can pin down the cause of vaginismus to one particular incident. A woman may have been sexually abused or her first experience of sex may have been painful for some reason, e.g. an unskilled lover or a particularly tough hymen, or she may have been brought up to have 'bad' feelings about her body and sex. The trouble with many sexual problems is that they tend to get into a vicious cycle where every time you try to have sex you become more anxious and (in this case literally) uptight and the situation gets worse. That makes you even more fearful of the next occasion and so it goes on.

Women suffering from severe vaginismus usually can't put anything inside their vagina at all. One of the first questions a therapist would ask them is whether they can use tampons or not. Usually they'll say they've tried but found it impossible so have always managed without. If you think that you are suffering from vaginismus then here are some things that you can try to help you get over it.

1. Read the chapter on 'Sex – the mechanics and the fun' and try to fit what I've written about a woman's body to your own body. Choose a time when you're feeling calm and can be private and have a look between your legs with a mirror. Try to identify the different openings into your body as well as your labia and your clitoris. Just look and touch them gently. If it makes you feel anxious or scared, stop for a while and do some deep breathing. Ask yourself why you feel bad about doing this. Try to remember that it's your own body

and you have every right to look at it and touch it if you want.

2. Have a warm bath with whatever bath oil or foam relaxes you most. Soap yourself all over, from head to toe. Do it slowly, enjoying the contours of your own body. If you find yourself thinking 'I'm too bony' or 'I can't bear to look at this, I'm so fat' just stop for a while, shut your eyes and reassure yourself that it's your body and it's special and try to appreciate it for what it is.

3. Still in the bath, put your hand between your legs. Very gently try to locate your clitoris with one finger and then slide your finger downwards and backwards until you get to the entrance to your vagina. You may find at this time that your knees spring together so that your hand can't move any further. Just relax, breathe deeply and wait till you feel ready, then try again. Very gently try to put just the very tip of one finger into the entrance of your vagina. You will feel a fleshy wall. You may also feel slightly sore and uncomfortable. If this happens, try not to pull your finger out but just stay still and concentrate on the sensation. Does it really feel very bad? Once your first panic subsides you will almost certainly find that it's only mild discomfort and not pain and you will be able to cope with it.

4. You may have to practise the steps above several times before you can get this far but if you can manage it, you're doing very well indeed. Once you can get the tip of your finger just inside your vagina, try pushing it a little bit further in. You'll feel the vagina clenching tight round your finger. This is the ring of muscle round the outer part of the vagina which is causing all the problem.

Try very gently to push your finger further in. You won't damage yourself and you'll find that with gentle pressure, the walls of flesh will gradually give way until you can insert your finger an inch or so. Don't worry if it takes a long time. You'll get there in the end.

5. With your finger still in there (this involves a bit of doubling up in the bath and you may at this stage want to transfer the exercise back on to dry land) try to imagine that you're passing urine and you want to stop the flow. You may want to practise this when you're sitting on the loo, although you don't actually have to pee to do it. When you do this, you tighten the muscle that controls the end of your vagina. It's like a pulling and lifting sensation in your lower pelvis. Try it now and see if you can twitch that muscle 'shut'. If you do it with your finger inside your vagina, you'll feel that muscle grip on to your finger. That's fine, it won't hurt your vagina or your finger. Clench that muscle as tight as you can and really grip on to your finger. You'll find that you can't do it for more than a few seconds, so then relax.

   Then clench again and relax and so on and so on. Gradually you learn to be able to control the muscle and the harder you clench the more you're able to relax in between clenches. Once you've got the idea of it with your finger inside your vagina, you can do it without your finger. Practise as often as possible. You can even do it when you're standing in the queue for a bus or drying the dishes in the kitchen; no one will know what you're up to unless you tell them.

6. For the rest of the exercises you need to be in a sexual relationship or at least in a relationship that you both want to become sexual. It's important that you tell your partner what's going on and ask for his help because he's going to need to be patient and caring. Perhaps you could let him read this bit in the book.

   Now allow your partner to put the tip of his finger inside your vagina. It'll be much easier if you do it gently after a lot of kissing and hugging and loveplay and you may want to hold on to his wrist so that you can pull his finger out at any time you want. He should also moisten the end of his finger with some spit or KY jelly to make it go in more easily. Practise your clenching and relaxing against him. After he has done this with one finger, you could try with two fingers.

7. Finally, if you both want to try it, you're ready to have intercourse. Again this isn't just a clinical exercise. It's something that should come after gentle lovemaking and foreplay when you both feel aroused. What you have to do is repeat the exercise above only using his penis instead of a finger. Remember to make sure that you are fixed up with contraception and also to use lots and lots of lubrication on his penis. Even if he's wearing a sheath, which normally has a spermicidal lubricant added to it, you or he could put some spit or some KY jelly (not Vaseline in this case because it can rot sheaths) round the entrance to your vagina.

    It's easier if he lies on his back and you kneel above him. That way, you control the depth of penetration and you can gently lower yourself on to him and raise yourself off again. One of you will have to hold his penis and guide it into the right hole. Contrary to many people's beliefs, penises aren't guided missiles and don't home in on targets on their own.

8. Congratulations, you made it. Well done, don't you feel proud of yourself?

    If you follow these points carefully and slowly with the help of a sympathetic and loving partner, you should be able to overcome your problems. But if not, don't despair. There are people around who can help you and the best thing is to go either on your own or with your partner to a psychosexual counsellor. More about this at the end of the chapter.

Can't reach an orgasm

Some women reach orgasm on their first experience of masturbation or lovemaking and others never, ever have one but spend their lives worrying about it. Whether you do reach a climax or not doesn't really matter as long as you enjoy your lovemaking and your relationship. You should certainly never feel guilty because you aren't having an orgasm and an understanding partner should never put pressure on you to 'achieve' one.

It's worth bearing in mind the following points about orgasm.

SEXUAL PROBLEMS

1. No one can 'give you' an orgasm. They can supply the necessary stimulation and lead you to it, but unless you are mentally and physically relaxed enough to reach that climax, they could be the greatest and most skilled lover in the world and you still wouldn't have one.

2. Just as no one else can 'give you' an orgasm, so you can't force yourself to have one. Many women complain that however hard they try, they just can't seem to get there. But it's precisely because they're trying so hard that they can't do it. An orgasm is a total release of tension and in order for that to happen you have to be able to let go both of your body and your mind. Some women find this very hard indeed. They cannot bear the feeling of being out of control. They say that they almost reach orgasm and then it's as though they step outside their bodies and start looking at themselves, not particularly liking what they see. Again this might be something to do with years of associating guilt with sex or it may just be that they're particularly self-conscious about their bodies and how they use them. Either way, the problem can be overcome once you become aware of it.

If you have this problem and you want to explore your own body to see if you can reach an orgasm then you may find the following suggestions helpful.

1. Get to know your body first. If you don't already masturbate, now is the time to start. Don't settle down with gritted teeth determined to reach an orgasm or die, just relax and accept that you're going to take some time exploring your own body.

2. Choose a time when you can be private and relaxed. This usually means in your bed at night or shut in the bathroom in the bath.

3. Remember what I said about physical and mental stimulation both being necessary for sexual arousal. You have to get in the right mood first. Often you can achieve this by thinking of some romantic or sexy story, or imagining yourself making

love to your favourite singer or actor. Lie back, close your eyes and think about it. This is called fantasy and it's a wonderful way of helping yourself relax enough to become aroused. You can even use it when you're making love with your partner. It's not cheating or unfair; just an extra dimension in lovemaking.

4. Slowly start to explore your body. Don't put your hands straight between your legs; stroke your shoulders, your arms and your breasts first of all. Concentrate on what your skin feels like in the different areas. Think about the contours and the way your fingers are going up and down over them. This is good practice for learning to make love to someone else as well!

   If you want to, you can use some baby oil or talcum powder to help your hands move softly over yourself. Try to imagine your body as a map and work out which areas should be shaded red for no go (doesn't give you much pleasure or feels nasty), green for yes (feels good) or amber for okay.

5. Gradually start to touch your inner thighs and gently stroke your fingers towards your vaginal lips. Wet one of your fingers with some spit or KY jelly and gently slide it in between the lips. Find your clitoris and rub around it gently. Slide your finger in and out of your vagina. As you become more aroused you'll find that the vagina and its entrance becomes wet. You're doing well.

6. It's now up to you to discover what feels best. You may find that your mind starts to wander. Try to pull it back. Keep it focused on what's happening. Concentrate on the sensations in your body and your fingers. But remember that the object of this is to give yourself pleasure. It doesn't matter whether or not you have an orgasm at the end. You can stop at any time you want to. Only do what feels good.

7. If you choose to carry on, and as you become more practised, you may feel yourself building up towards a climax. As I said before this is rather like the holding of breath before a sneeze. Sometimes women begin to feel it coming and then it just

slips out of reach. There are a few tricks that you can try to help bring it closer. One is to flex your body and spread your legs out and hold them taut until it almost hurts. Hanging your head backwards over the edge of a bed or just lying back and trying to arch your back also increases the tension and brings climax that bit closer.

If you try these steps out gradually at your own pace there's a good chance that you'll eventually achieve orgasm. Once you know what it feels like, and more importantly, understand the kind of stimulation you need to get there, it's up to you to teach your partner. Remember that men aren't automatically wonderful lovers. They aren't born knowing what feels good to a woman. And all women are different anyway so even if they learnt with one it could be different for another. Help them to discover the ways to unlock your pleasure. Ask them to show you what feels good to them in turn. If you don't feel able to talk about it then just take their hands and show them. Don't be scared that you'll turn a man off like this; he'll be thrilled that you enjoy your own body enough to want to share it with him.

Common male problems

Pain on erection or intercourse

If you experience pain when your penis becomes erect or when you have sex, or if there is any bleeding from the penis, you should consult your GP. I know it's very embarrassing talking to your doctor about things like this but it's important that you give him a chance to rule out any physical problems. You may have a slight infection that a course of antibiotics would clear up and it's always better to get this seen to rather than go on risking pain and discomfort and possibly infecting your partner with something she'd rather not have.

Sometimes pain on erection is caused by a tight foreskin. It may be that you have trouble pulling it back during masturbation or during sex or it could be that once it's been pulled back it can't go forward again very easily. If you have this problem then try gently pulling your foreskin backwards and forwards with soap and water once a day. During a bath or a shower is the obvious time. Doing this for a couple of weeks will quite likely solve the problem but if it doesn't you must see your doctor. Many men are terrified that they'd have to have a circumcision, but it often isn't necessary. It may be caused by a swelling due to an infection or it may just be that the foreskin needs loosening. This is a very simple procedure and although it's mainly done under general anaesthetic, it's nothing like as drastic as a circumcision.

Finally, if you ever get stuck in a position where your foreskin pulls back then can't go forward again and your penis stays erect and swollen and painful, you MUST seek medical help straightaway. This is dangerous and it will not get better of its own accord.

Coming too quickly

Coming too quickly or the feeling of not being able to hold off ejaculation (medical term – premature ejaculation) is something that happens to all men at some time. It's more common in a younger man and nearly always happens the first few times they try to make love or the first time they make love in any particular relationship. It's caused by over excitement. Unfortunately, there's then the vicious cycle affecting many sexual problems where the more anxious you become about it, the more uptight you'll be the next time and the more likely it is to repeat itself.

If you are sensible you can break out of this cycle early on by understanding that it's not your fault, but a perfectly natural occurrence. However, some men get caught in the cycle and find that they always ejaculate either before they can get their penis inside their partner's vagina or immediately upon penetration. They often become extremely worried and depressed about this and it can stop them from having anything to do with girls because they feel so ashamed of their problem.

Luckily premature ejaculation, like many other sexual problems, is fairly easily curable with the right advice and patient practice. The secret is learning to recognise the feeling in the body immediately before ejaculation. If you can be confident of knowing when you get to that point, you can damp down some of the stimulation so that you don't go over the top and climax. This gives you enough control to carry on for much, much longer.

Here are some exercises which might help.

1. Learn to control your climax on your own first before trying it out with a partner. Find yourself a quiet and private time and place to masturbate. Make sure you feel relaxed and get yourself in the mood by thinking your favourite sexy thoughts and fantasies or looking at magazines or pictures.

2. Try to masturbate almost to the point of orgasm. Just before you feel you're about to come, take your hands away and think about something else. Something that's so boring that it will take your mind right off sex. Often people can get hold of one particular mental picture which they use for this. It comes in very useful as a kind of psychological trigger telling your body to hold back.

3. Try to hold on to this thought and don't touch yourself. With luck your erection will wilt a little. Let that happen and after a minute or two go back and carry on masturbating.

4. Repeat it all over again. Get to the point where you almost climax and then hold off. Try to do this three or four times before reaching a climax.

5. Practise this several times a week. You won't get it right first time but with dedication it will sort itself out.

6. If you have a sexual partner you can then, with her help, try to put what you've learnt into practice. The best way is to tell her exactly what you're doing and show her this section in the book if you like. Ask her then to masturbate you. If she hasn't done this before you'll find it intensely exciting and you may well climax straightaway. That's okay. If it happens, rest for a while cuddling each other and wait until you feel ready to start again. Ask her to touch you in whatever way you like best but to stop as soon as you say. Use your mental turn-off picture, wait for a minute or two and carry on again. Try to build up to four or five times before reaching a climax.

7. When you can do this comfortably and happily it's time to try intercourse. The best position is with you lying on your back and her kneeling above you, lowering herself down on to your penis. She is in control but you have to say stop and go. Let her lower herself so that your penis goes inside her vagina (you may have to help it in) but as soon as you feel you're about to come, say stop and she should lift herself off and you should think of your mental turn-off picture. Again try to build this up to four or five times before you ejaculate.

8. Congratulations, you're there. You've finally got great control. Don't forget to thank your partner and to make sure that she enjoys lovemaking too!

Difficulty keeping an erection

Sometimes this is called impotence but what it really means is a man has trouble keeping his penis erect long enough to have sex. Many men may wish that their penis would stay erect indefinitely so that they could fulfil their 'Superstud' image but the man who truly suffers from this problem finds that his erection wilts as soon as he approaches the woman or starts to have intercourse.

It's not that he comes too quickly because he doesn't ejaculate at all, the erection just fades away.

Sometimes there's a physical cause for this. Alcohol is the best known one. A night of heavy drinking can often lead to disastrous or even humiliating attempts to make love to your partner. This is enough to make some men so anxious that the next time they try to have sex, the anxiety itself stops them being able to perform. If you have this problem ask yourself whether drink could be the cause. Some medically prescribed drugs also do it. If you are on a course of medical treatment and this suddenly starts to happen, it's worthwhile checking with your doctor whether the medicine could be the cause of it. Sometimes, but very, very rarely, problems with erection can be early warning symptoms of a more serious disease.

For this reason, if you can't get over the problem with time or by following the exercises below, it's always best to ask your doctor for advice. He may want to give you a physical check-up and even

SEXUAL PROBLEMS

if there is no medical cause for it he'll be able to refer you on to someone who can help you.

So what do you do if you have a problem with a wilting erection? Well, first of all, you have to bear in mind that old vicious cycle again. The more anxious you are, the less likely it is you'll be able to perform. And the more you have trouble performing the more anxious you'll become. The best way of coping with this is by following a course of exercises designed by psychosexual therapists called Sensate Focus. You can try these on your own i.e. by masturbation but they're really designed to be used by a couple. So if you're in a steady and loving relationship with a partner who you can trust enough to ask to help you with your problem, this is what you should do.

1. Agree that for the time being, maybe the next three or four weeks, you're not going to try and have intercourse. Make it a pact between the two of you. That immediately takes the pressure off you to perform.

2. What you do do instead is a series of graded exercises designed to explore each other's body and take you back to the very early sensual levels of foreplay. For these exercises you need to be somewhere alone, warm, comfortable and private. You need to be relaxed enough to take your clothes off and lie down together without fear of anyone knocking at the door or rushing into the room. It's a good idea for you both to have a relaxing bath beforehand. Remembering that you're not going to have intercourse, you spend the first couple of sessions gradually exploring each other's bodies. One of you lies down and the other kneels beside them and very gently and carefully strokes and touches them from head to toe. However, you do not touch either breasts or genitals. It's as though there's an invisible no-go area drawn round the breasts and between the legs.

   While you're doing this both of you should concentrate on the sensations that you can feel either while it's being done to you or through your fingers as you touch and stroke your partner. If other thoughts start to come into your mind, try to push them out and go back and concentrate very hard again on just what you're doing. Often, you'll find that you touch different parts of your partner, parts you've never touched before. Have you ever stroked or licked them between their toes? So long as they haven't got smelly feet both of you will either like it or hate it.

Allow 15–20 minutes each and afterwards cuddle up together and talk about how it felt. Tell each other which bits you liked touching the most and where you enjoyed being stroked best.

3. After you've done this several times you can move on to do the same exercise including the breasts and the genitals. But remember, you aren't going to have intercourse. This is purely to enjoy each other's bodies, to give pleasure and to receive pleasure. This exercise is often dramatically successful in helping couples get closer together and it's quite an eye opener to see how much pleasure someone gets from touching you.

4. The chances are that if you are feeling safe and secure enough the exercise above will cause you to have an erection. After you've repeated this several times you can decide that this time you're going to go ahead and try to put your penis inside your partner's vagina. But the object isn't to have an orgasm or full intercourse; purely to extend the body contact to that closest contact of all, the penis inside the vagina. Do your stroking and your touching and your hugging gradually focusing in on the genitals. Then as an extension of this, try to put your penis inside your partner or ask her to kneel above you lowering herself down on you. Just hold it there, feel the sensations, and withdraw.

If you followed all the steps above successfully then you've done it, you've beaten your problem. You can now go ahead, do everything as above, and carry on until you reach orgasm. The great bonus is that once you've done it once, you realise that you are capable of doing it and the problem will probably disappear overnight.

And finally:

We never seem to come at the same time

I've got news for you. It's only in story books that people reach their orgasm at the same time. If you've got this far in the book and you still think that most women reach their climax by a man pumping away with his penis and doing nothing else then you haven't been paying attention! The majority of women need direct clitoral stimulation to reach orgasm and because of that many of them can only reach it before or after their partners have had their climax inside their vagina. Even those that do reach orgasm during 'straight intercourse' are still quite likely not to get there at the exact same moment as their partner.

AND IT DOESN'T MATTER. You're both giving and receiving pleasure. Orgasm itself is an intensely lonely experience because you cut yourself off from everything that's going on around you. If you both reach that point, at the same moment, all the time, you would never have the pleasure of seeing your partner reach their orgasm.

Getting help

Until recently, it was quite difficult to get help for sexual problems. GPs often didn't like talking about sex very much and, to be honest, often didn't know all that much about it! However, nowadays they're much more aware of sexuality and its problems and there are also far more clinics where you can be referred or go along to.

If you have a sexual problem and the suggestions so far haven't been able to help you then there are several ways you can get further help.

1. You can approach your GP and ask him/her if he will refer you to a psychosexual counsellor or clinic. You don't necessarily have to tell him what the problem is in great detail. You could say that you'd rather not talk about it with him but could he refer you on. Most GPs will do this and most major cities have a psychosexual clinic attached to one of their hospitals. Alternatively, your GP may know of a private

counsellor or an NHS psychologist who takes on psychosexual cases.

2. RELATE (The Marriage Guidance Council) also runs special psychosexual counselling clinics. You can find details of your nearest one either by contacting your local branch (look in the phone book under Marriage Guidance) or by asking their head office for further information. See the address in the 'Contacts' section. Like the NHS clinics above, these counsellors are just as happy to see you young or old, married or single.

3. You can ask your family planning clinic doctor or nurse for help. Many of them are very skilled at advising on sexual problems but even if not they will have suggestions as to where you can go for help. They're often able to refer you directly to psychosexual clinics without going through your GP.

4. You can find private, individual psychosexual counsellors or therapists. However, be warned that anyone can call themselves a counsellor or therapist or sex therapist without having any qualifications at all. They may be well meaning but some of them are dangerous. The best way of getting in touch with a qualified and reputable counsellor or therapist is to ask the British Association of Counselling to help you. If you write to them with a very brief description of your type of problem and the area you live in, enclosing an s.a.e. of course, they'll give you some suggestions of who and where you can contact.

Sex and disability

Emotional and sexual relationships are tricky enough for an able-bodied person, so when you add the extra ingredient of a disability things can become very difficult. Part of this is due to the attitude of the rest of the world. You may find that your family and friends tend to be overprotective, making it hard for you to achieve the independence needed to form new relationships. You may also find that your disability itself makes it hard for prospective partners to view you in an equal light.

SEXUAL PROBLEMS

Fortunately the attitude of society, particularly the caring services part of it, is changing. Most professionals working with young disabled people are well aware that a minor or major physical or mental handicap doesn't stop the person inside the body having romantic and physical feelings. So while you may find that although adults don't bring up the subject of sex and relationships readily they're often very happy to help you out with problems once you initiate the discussion.

Some areas of handicap obviously cause particular problems with sexual relationships and, if bits of your body don't work, you may think that it's impossible ever to have sex. But you would almost certainly be wrong. We tend to forget that our whole body is a sexual organ and capable of high levels of arousal, so, even if there is a lack of feeling and response in the more obvious sexual bits you can often find that other areas of the body become important pleasure centres. And when it comes to the physical act of intercourse there are a variety of aids and therapies available to make the impossible happen.

For more information and confidential advice on any of these areas see the addresses in the 'Contacts' section.

Contacts

Local help groups and services are often listed in the phone book and *Thomson Directory*. Libraries are also a good source of information and they keep lists of all local services. You can ring up to find out what's available.

Most of the following organisations are based in London or other large cities but they will usually be able to put you in touch with agencies in other parts of the country. Ring them or send an s.a.e. for details.

General advice and counselling

Benefits Agency
Freephone 0800 666555
For general (not personal claim) advice on all benefits.

British Association for Counselling
1 Regent Place, Rugby, Warwickshire CV21 2PJ
Send a stamped addressed envelope for details of counselling organisations and qualified private counsellors in your area. They deal with all different types of recognised counselling including sexual problems.

Childline
Freephone 0800 1111
24-hour confidential advice service for young people.

Children's Legal Centre
20 Compton Terrace, London N1 2UN
Tel: 071-359 6251

Citizens Advice Bureaux
Look in the phone book to find your nearest one and ring for opening hours. Gives free and confidential advice on all sorts of subjects, including where to go for further help.

CONTACTS

NSPCC Helpline
Freephone 0800 800 500
24-hour helpline for children and young people – or anyone concerned about the safety of a child or young person.

Redwood Women's Training Association
5 Spennithorn Road, Skellow, Doncaster, South Yorkshire DN6 8PF
0302 337151
Nationwide organisation offering group courses in assertiveness and/or sexuality.

The Samaritans
Branches in every town in the country. Look in the phone book under *Samaritans* or dial 100 for the operator and ask to be connected. They offer a sympathetic ear around the clock for anyone with a problem, large or small. There's face-to-face counselling as well as help over the phone.

Social Work Departments
Look in the phone book under *Social Services* for nearest office. Ring to make an appointment or walk in and ask to see the Duty Social Worker. Can give help on family and accommodation problems as well as practical help and advice on pregnancy.

Youth Access
Magazine Business Centre, 11 Newarke Street, Leicester LE1 5SS
This central office acts as a referral agency for youth counselling services all over the country. Send s.a.e. for details of one nearest you.

Making friends

National Federation of 18-Plus Groups
Nicholson House, Old Court Road, Newent, Gloucestershire GL18 1AG
Tel: 0531 821210

PHAB
(Clubs for physically handicapped and able bodied young people)
12–14 London Road, Croydon CR0 2TA
Tel: 081–680 6939

Roteract (18–28 years) and **Interact** (14–18 years)
c/o Rotary International, Kinwarton Road, Alcester, Warwickshire B49 6BP
Tel: 0789 765411

Youth Clubs UK
11 St Bride Street, London EC4A 4AS
Tel: 071–353 2366

Gays, lesbians and sexual identity problems

The Albany Trust
Sunra Centre, 26 Balham Hill, London SW12 9EB Tel: 081–675 6669
Offers counselling for all types of relationship and sexual identity problems. Branches in London, Birmingham, Brighton, Bristol, Guildford and Hove.

Identity Counselling
Marylebone Counselling Centre, 17 Marylebone Road, London NW1 5LT
Tel: 071–487 3797 – 1–4 p.m. Mon, Tues, Wed and Fri, 2.15–4.15 p.m. Thurs.
Offers help and counselling to anyone worried about their sexual identity.

Lesbian and Gay Switchboard
BM Switchboard, London WC1N 3XX
Tel: 071–837 7324
24-hour information and help for lesbians and gays. Other switchboards operate all over the country, look in local press for details or ring London switchboard and ask for your local number.

Lesbian and Gay Youth Movement
LGYB, BM/GYM, London WC1N 3XX
Tel: 081–317 9690 – Fridays 6–9 p.m.
Can refer you to local Gay Youth movements all over the country. Enclose s.a.e.

London Friend
86 Caledonian Road, London N1 9DN
Tel: 071–837 3337 (evening helpline); 071–837 2782 (women's Tues and Thurs evening Helpline)
Offers counselling and support for lesbians or any woman who is worried about her sexual identity.

Parents' Friend
c/o 36 Newmarket, Otley, W. Yorks LS21 3AE
Tel: 0532 674627
Organisation for parents of gays, lesbians and bi-sexuals.

Relationships and sexual problems

Brook Advisory Centres
153 East Street, London SE17 2SD
Tel: 071–708 1234
Offers counselling to young people with relationship and sexual problems as well as family planning advice and help with unwanted pregnancies. Branches in London, Birmingham, Bristol, Edinburgh, Liverpool, Burnley and Belfast, with new Centres opening each year. Telephone above number for details of your nearest Centre.

Marriage Counselling Scotland
26 Frederick Street, Edinburgh EH2 2JR
Tel: 031-225 5006
Can refer you to local Marriage Guidance services or look in the phone book under *Marriage Guidance*. Offers counselling to individuals and couples, married or single, with relationship problems. Some areas offer psychosexual counselling clinics.

RELATE (National Marriage Guidance Council)
Little Church Street, Rugby CV21 3AP
Tel: 0788 573241
As above but for England, Wales and Northern Ireland.

Resolve
PO Box 820, London N10 3AW
Support group for vaginismus sufferers

Family planning, pregnancy advice and abortion

British Pregnancy Advisory Service (BPAS)
Austey Manor, Wootton Wawen, Solihull, West Midlands B95 6BX
Tel: 0564 793225
Reputable charity offering advice and counselling on pregnancy (including unwanted pregnancy and abortion), infertility, sexual problems and sterilisation. Twenty-six branches nationwide and five nursing homes.

Family Planning Association
27-35 Mortimer Street, London W1N 7JR
Tel: 071-636 7866
Information on all FP Clinics in the UK as well as all aspects of family planning and sexual health. Write with s.a.e. for free leaflets or ring Monday to Friday 11 a.m. to 3.30 p.m.

LIFE
Life House, Newbold Terrace, Leamington Spa, Warwickshire CV32 4EA
Helpline 0926 311511, open between 9 a.m. and 9 p.m.
Offers counselling and practical help to women with unplanned pregnancy. Some accommodation available for homeless pregnant women and unsupported mothers with babies. Ring head office for details or look in local phone book under *LIFE*.
NB It should be noted that LIFE is an anti-abortion charity and therefore does not recommend abortion as an option.

Marie Stopes House
The Well Woman Centre
108 Whitfield Street, London W1P 6BE
Tel: 071-388 0662/2585

Offers counselling and information on women's sexual health, including contraception and pregnancy. Also has branches in Leeds and Manchester.

Post Abortion Counselling Service
340 Westbourne Park Road, London W11 1EQ
071-221 9631

Pregnancy Advisory Service
13 Charlotte Street, London W1P 1HD
Tel: 071-637 8962
Counselling and help for women with unwanted pregnancies as well as regular Well Woman checks. Offers post-abortion counselling.

Society for the Protection of the Unborn Child
7 Tufton Street, London SW1P 4QN
Tel: 071-222 5845; Scotland 041-221 2094; Northern Ireland 0232 778018
SPUC offers free educational services and runs educational campaigns to inform people about the humanity of the unborn child and effects of abortion on baby and mother. Also information on population growth and experimentation on human embryos.

Single parents

See page 129 for LIFE, which offers a lot of help and support.

Gingerbread
35 Wellington Street, London WC2E 7BN
Tel: 071-240 0953
Has over 300 self-help groups for single-parent families all over the country.

National Council for One-Parent Families
255 Kentish Town Road, London NW5 2LX
Tel: 071-267 1361
Offers free advice to single-parent families and single pregnant women about the law, housing facilities, support services, etc.

Rape and incest

Childline
Freephone 0800 1111
24-hour confidential advice service for young people.

NSPCC Helpline
Freephone 0800 800 500
24-hour helpline for children and young people – or anyone concerned about the safety of a child or young person.

Rape Crisis Centres
PO Box 69, London WC1X 9NJ
Tel: 071–837 1600
Confidential counselling for rape victims. Volunteers may be able to accompany you to report incident to the police. Branches in London, Belfast, Cardiff, Dublin and Edinburgh.

AIDS

National AIDS Helpline
Freephone 0800 567123

Positively Healthy
PO Box 71, Richmond, Surrey TW9 3DJ
081–878 6443
Self-help group encouraging a positive approach to coping with HIV or AIDS.

Positively Women
5 Sebastian Street, London EC1V 0HE
071–490 5515 from 10 a.m. to 5 p.m.
Women offering support, counselling and information to women with HIV or AIDS.

Terrence Higgins Trust
52–54 Grays Inn Road, London WC1X 8JU
Helpline 071–242 1010 – 3–10 p.m. daily
Legal Line 071–405 2381 – 7–10 p.m. Wed

Drugs

ADFAM
18 Hatton Place, London EC1N 8ND
Tel: 071–405 3923 – 10 a.m.–5 p.m. weekdays
National service for families and friends of drug users, offering counselling, details of local drug services around the UK and accurate information on drugs.

RELEASE
388 Old Street, London EC1V 9LT
Tel: 071–729 9904
Offers advice and referral on drug and legal problems and emergency help in cases of arrest.

Alcohol

ACCEPT Services UK
724 Fulham Road, London SW6 5SE
Tel: 071-371 7477
Promotes education, training and preventative measures connected with alcohol misuse. Runs a treatment centre and offers counselling.

Alateen
Al-Anon Family Groups UK and Eire, 61 Great Dover Street, London SE1 4YF
24-hour telephone 071-403 0888
For young people whose lives have been affected by someone else's drinking. Also **Al-Anon** which offers support to families and friends of alcoholics.

Alcohol Concern
275 Grays Inn Road, London WC1X 8QF
Tel: 071-833 3471

Turning Point
New Loom House, 101 Back Church Lane, London E1 1LU
Tel: 071-702 2300
Deals with drug and mental health problems in addition to alcohol problems.

Disability and sex

SPOD (Sexual Problems of the Disabled)
286 Camden Road, London N7 0BJ
Tel: 071-607 8851
SPOD is a small organisation with limited office hours and you may have to ring several times before getting through.

RADAR (Royal Association for Disability and Rehabilitation)
25 Mortimer Street, London W1N 8AB
Tel: 071-637 5400
RADAR does not itself provide counselling but it is sympathetic and can refer you to appropriate local services.

Outsiders Club
PO Box 4ZB, London W1A 4ZB
Social and campaigning group for the disabled.

PHAB
(Clubs for physically handicapped and able-bodied young people)
12-14 London Road, Croydon CR0 2TA
Tel: 081-680 6939

CANADA

Alcoholics Anonymous
Toronto Intergroup Officer, 234 Eglington Avenue East, Suite 502, Toronto, Ontario, M4P 1K5
Tel: 416 487 5591
The Toronto office can refer you to AA groups in different cities or you can check in your phone book for your local intergroup office.

AIDS Committee of Ottawa – Support and Information Line
Tel: 613 238 4111

Canadian AIDS Society
100 Sparks Street, Suite 701, Ottawa, Ontario, K1P 5B7
Tel: 613 230 3580

The Ontario Coalition for Abortion Clinics
PO Box 753, Station P, Toronto, Ontario, M5S 2Z1
Tel: 416 789 4541

Planned Parenthood Federation of Canada
1 Nicholus Street, Suite 430, Ottawa, Ontario, K1N 7B7
Tel: 613 238 4474
Can refer you to local centres for information and advice on contraception and sexuality.

NEW ZEALAND

Local phone books often list counselling services at the beginning of the directory.

AIDS Toll-free Hotline – 0800 802 437

New Zealand AIDS Foundation (National Office)
PO Box 6663, Wellesley Street, Auckland

New Zealand Family Planning Association (National Office)
PO Box 11515, Wellington
Tel: (04) 384 4349
Can refer you to local services for advice and information.

AUSTRALIA

For counselling and family planning services look first of all in the section at the beginning of your telephone directory.
The following organisations can also refer you to local services:

CONTACTS

The Abortion and Contraception Advisory Service
116 Wellington Parade, East Melbourne, Victoria 3002
Tel: 03 419 1686

Family Planning Association New Territories
Shop 11, Rapid Creek Shopping Centre, Trower Road, Rapid Creek, NT 08 10
Tel: 089 480 144

Family Planning Association of Queensland
100 Alfred Street, Fortitude Valley, Queensland 4006
Tel: 07 252 5151

Family Planning Association of South Australia
17 Phillips Street, Kensington, SA 5068
Tel: 08 315 177

Family Planning Association of Tasmania
73 Federal Street, PO Box 77, North Hobart, Tasmania 7002
Tel: 002 347 200

Family Planning Association of Victoria
259 Church Street, Richmond, Victoria 3121
Tel: 03 429 1868

Family Planning Federation of Australia
Health Promotion Centre, Childers Street, Canberra ACT 2601
Tel: 06 247 3077

Health Sharing Women
Health Information Query Line. Tel: 03 663 3544

Western Australia AIDS Council
107 Brisbane Street, Northbridge, Western Australia 6000
Tel: 09 227 8355

Western Institute of Self Help (WISH)
30 Railway Street, Cottesloe, Western Australia 6011
Tel: 09 383 3188
Offers help with addictions, sexually transmitted diseases and other health problems plus a complete referral list of self-help groups and local services.

The Women's Health Resource Collective
653 Nicholson Street, Carlton North, Victoria 3054
Tel: 03 380 9974 or toll-free 008 133 321

For information and advice you can also contact the Health Educator in your local Community Health Centre. They can give you free and confidential information on contraception, sexually transmitted diseases and other health matters as well as details of local family planning and counselling clinics. To find your nearest Community Health Centre contact your State Health Department, see below.

Victoria – Melbourne, tel: 03 616 7777
New South Wales – Sydney, tel: 02 391 9000
Queensland – Brisbane, tel: 07 234 0111
ACT – Canberra, tel: 06 205 5111
Western Australia – Perth, tel: 09 426 3444
South Australia – Adelaide, tel: 08 237 6111
Tasmania – Hobart, tel: 002 333 185
Northern Territory – Darwin, tel: 089 22 888

SOUTH AFRICA

AIDS Care
Tel: 011 425 2521

AIDS Training and Information Centres (ATIC)
Dial INFO national number 10118 for your local centre.

Gay Advice Bureau
Tel: 011 643 2311

Lifeline Johannesburg (South Transvaal)
PO Box 95135, Grant Park, Johannesburg 2051
Tel: 011 728 1347
This organisation has telephone counsellors and a data bank of individuals and organisations to whom people can be referred. They have branches all over South Africa.

Planned Parenthood Association of Southern Africa
3rd Floor, Marlborough House, 60 Eloff Street, Johannesburg 2001
Tel: 011 331 2695/2696/2697

Emergencies

In case of emergency look first of all at the 'Contacts' chapter (pages 126–35) for an appropriate counselling or advice agency.
You may also find the following list useful:

When your relationship breaks up, 53

Losing your virginity, 63–4

Contraception
  getting it, 68–71
  emergency/morning after contraception, 77–8

Think you're pregnant? 80–5

Your girlfriend's pregnant, 85–6

Abortion, 86–9

Sexually transmitted diseases and other
    sexual health problems, 96–100

Painful sex
  female, 103–7
  male, 110–11

Sexual problems – getting help, 116–17

HIV tests, 122